THE ARMCHAIR MILLIONAIRE

The
Armchair
Millionaire

....

Lewis Schiff

and

Douglas Gerlach

POCKET BOOKS
New York London Toronto Sydney Singapore

This publication is designed to provide accurate and authoritative information in regard to the subject matter covered. It is sold with the understanding that neither the author nor the publisher is engaged in rendering legal, investment, accounting, or other professional services. If legal advice or other expert assistance is required, the services of a competent professional person should be sought.

 POCKET BOOKS, a division of Simon & Schuster, Inc.
1230 Avenue of the Americas, New York, NY 10020

ISBN: 0-7434-1191-9

First Pocket Books hardcover printing April 2001

10 9 8 7 6 5 4 3 2 1

POCKET and colophon are registered trademarks of Simon & Schuster, Inc.

Designed by Lindgren/Fuller Design

Printed in the U.S.A.

To my family, who made it so easy for me to be whatever I wanted.
To Lynette, who has made it all worth it.
LEWIS SCHIFF

To the memory of my father,
who taught me to respect others as well as myself.
To A.M., who was a great friend when I needed it most.
DOUGLAS GERLACH

ACKNOWLEDGMENTS

This book is the product of an entire community of investing enthusiasts, supporters, and volunteers, in both the virtual and the physical world.

Many thanks go to the original Armchair Millionaire supporters. Without a doubt John Bowen and Robert Levitan top that list. Many professionals lent much more than their expertise, including Dan Ambrose, Geoffrey Menin, Jim Safka, Pamela Saunders, and Richard Laermer.

Two teams helped us make the Armchair Millionaire real: The first team included Walston Bobb-Semple, Jr., Alex Knowlton, Katie Soden, and Gary Wiebke.

The second team has joined our game since then: Amanda Meffert, Tony Morelli, Jill Schwartz, Barry Hoggard and his tech squad, Amit Gupta, Matt Potosnak, and David Wagenheim.

Agent Bob Levine and Pocket Books president Judith Curr believed in this book . . . twice! Thanks and thanks again.

Jimmy Fitzgerald, Bill Karsh, and Craig Goldberg, you've given much more than you've gotten in return (so far).

To Albert Wenger and the crew at Launch Center 39, thank you for all your help and support.

From Lewis:

Thank you to the influential people who said "yes" at just the right time: Randy Jones of *Worth* for allowing me to put his magazine online even before I knew what I was doing; and Scott Cook, founder of Intuit, for letting me put ArmchairMillionaire.com on Quicken.com when it was just an idea.

Our biggest thanks must go to the members of the Armchair Millionaire community, who are the real heroes of our story. They make every day a day closer to financial freedom for themselves and for each other.

CONTENTS

INTRODUCTION

LEWIS SCHIFF

Investing is a lot like buying a car. As a consumer, you've got many choices, but there's no such thing as the "best" choice for everyone, only the one that's right for you. Some folks are looking for speed. Others want safety. Still others don't care what they drive, so long as it gets them there.

There are so many choices in the car market, with not a great deal of difference between them, that the manufacturers and marketers rely on hype to convince prospective customers of the superiority of one model over another. It's gotten so bad that even if one of these companies actually managed to create a truly great product, it would be difficult for car buyers to know.

Once you've decided you want a minivan rather than an SUV, you're still faced with a bewildering choice of vehicles. In reality, a minivan is a minivan is a minivan. One model isn't all that different from another. This is where marketers come in, filling magazines, newspapers, and airwaves with so much hoopla that you don't know what to believe anymore.

In the face of all that, you will eventually make a car choice because a car, for most of us, is an essential tool for living. Unfortunately, beginning your investing plan often doesn't have the same

priority. Given what you have to go through to start an investing program, I completely understand why.

With all that noise—experts offering conflicting advice on what
to do, stock markets and interest rates going up and down, new
economy stocks replacing old blue chips, and thousands of mutual
funds and brokers to choose from—investing can seem like a risky
proposition. That's too bad, because a solid investment strategy is
every bit as crucial as a car. And it will certainly get you farther than
a car ever could.

I was lucky. I was a nerd who was drawn to investing at an early
age—not because I come from a family of savers or investors and
not because I am in love with numbers. What drew me to investing
was that, like a puzzle, it seemed so complicated on the surface that
I had to get inside and figure it out.

My interest in investing dates back to my very first job. As a
fourteen-year-old, I worked on Wall Street one summer as a messenger for an international investment bank. My grandfather got me the
job (he was a messenger, too). As I sped from tower to tower, deliv-
ering packages, I sensed that there was less to Wall Street than met
the eye.

About a decade later, I ended up working at a financial magazine—not as a reporter, but as a computer consultant. My job was to
use technology to make magazine production more cost effective. I
had been bitten by the investing bug a few years earlier, and now I
wanted to get inside the industry to see how it worked. My upbring-
ing as a skeptic led me not to Wall Street this time but to a magazine, where I imagined I'd find out how investing and stock markets
really worked, not how "the Street" said they worked.

What I learned at the magazine was very disappointing. It was no
different than other parts of the financial industry. Investing professionals, whether they are journalists or stockbrokers, are paid to act
as interpreters for their readers or customers. In that sense, the
more you know, the less you need them. So they rely on a constant
river of complex ideas and alluring possibilities to keep you coming

back—from biotechnology stocks to investment trusts to mortgage-backed securities.

The World Wide Web changed all that. The interactive nature of the Web allows investors to "talk" to each other in a way that they never could have before. This directly challenges the broker-client relationship. In tiny virtual communities, people share the ideas that have really worked for them—ideas that are making them wealthy, ideas that are not very difficult to understand. In fact, they make a lot of common sense.

I began the Armchair Millionaire Web site because I knew—along with a great many other people—that investing intelligently doesn't have to be complicated. Thus the world's first commonsense savings and investing community was born.

There are at least tens of thousands of Armchair Millionaires, and probably a whole lot more than that. We have ordinary incomes, but our portfolios have done extraordinarily well. We don't have super-computers in our homes to analyze data, and we don't eat cat food in order to save money to invest. We lead normal lives.

Well, we may stand out in a few ways. We are patient and we are disciplined. We understand the dangers of easy credit—too often from experience. We found out how to invest successfully on our own because we are "do-it-yourselfer" types who need to know how and why things work before we jump into them. We are skeptics, but not cynics. Our goal is financial independence but our expectations are realistic. Most important, we are all either millionaires or on our way to becoming millionaires.

How simple is it? Well, I don't want to exaggerate. There are a few new ideas that are going to sound foreign at first. There's also new terminology that you will need to learn.

And then there's the financial services industry.

They are not crazy about simple, commonsense investing strategies. There is a prevailing wisdom out there, whether you hear it at a cocktail party or from your uncle, the stockbroker, that investing is a macho game in which you are judged not by how well you do for yourself, but by how much better you do compared to those around you. These folks tell you that you need to be in the "top performing" fund or that they've found the next Microsoft—"Get in while you can!"

The fact is, the successful investors who make up the Armchair Millionaire community are more interested in reaching their long-term goals than in attracting a crowd at a cocktail party. They also know that there are several factors that affect your long-term portfolio's performance—and the increase in value of your investments is just one of them. Spending as little as possible on fees and commissions is another.

And so, the tools you need to implement this commonsense investing strategy—we call it the Armchair Millionaire's Five Steps to Financial Freedom—are not available at every bank or brokerage. But they are available at the some of the biggest firms (we'll tell you which in Chapter 8, "Use the Armchair Investing Strategy"). More and more companies are realizing the value of the long-term investor each day. In fact, there's been something of a revolution in the past decade, wherein the investor on Main Street has gained access to the kinds of investing tools and information that used to be available only to the super-wealthy and to institutional investors. We'll show you how to benefit from that revolution and navigate through the brokerage world to get the most services while spending the least in fees.

Of course, there's much more to becoming an Armchair Millionaire than just implementing the Five Steps to Financial Freedom. While the steps are simple in and of themselves—we've laid out each step for you in this book—they require a certain degree of emotional intelligence, too. Patience and discipline are an Armchair Millionaire's key to realizing investing success and financial independence.

The books on investing that line shelf after shelf at your local bookstore will try to tell you that successful investing is complicated. Armchair Millionaires realize that these books may make for interesting reading, but they aren't required to build a sophisticated portfolio.

That's what makes this book different from all those other books—Armchair Millionaires say that investing isn't about complicated formulas, or anything else that's complicated. This book will show you, step by step, how to invest successfully. It includes simple, clear, straightforward investing advice for people in every stage of life. We will show you which investments to buy, how much, and when.

In these pages you'll hear investing wisdom from a wide variety of people—from the most prominent investing giants in history to individual investors who may be a lot like you. They'll describe their enthusiasm for these very simple concepts. Shutting off the noise and relying on common sense is the thread that runs through their stories. They will share their own investing experiences with you in this book as they do on the Armchair Millionaire Web site each day in our forums, bulletin boards, surveys, and other community events.

Listen to these folks. You'll find out that there is a "best" way to invest for most people. It's simple, easy to implement, and powerful enough to help most of us achieve financial independence.

So, whether you are deep in debt, a nincompoop about money, or hopelessly pressed for time, don't despair. You'll find someone in this book with a similar predicament. The only difference between them and you is that they have put these five commonsense investing steps into action, and now they've accomplished what they previously believed was near impossible. Think of them as the "after" and yourself as the "before."

Best of all, their wisdom and support are available to you twenty-four hours a day for no charge (except for the cost of hooking up to the Internet). At the Armchair Millionaire's online community, you've got a sounding board, a research tool, a place to get inspiration, and a whole group of friends who share a very important priority—financial freedom.

Please let me know how you fare on your own journey to financial independence. I'm at lewis@armchairmillionaire.com and I'd love to welcome you to our commonsense investing community.

Part I

....

Getting Ready
for the Journey

CHAPTER 1

What Is an Armchair Millionaire?

"You don't need a million bucks to be an Armchair Millionaire!"

When you visit Armchair Millionaire on the Web (www.armchairmillionaire. com), you'll see this phrase scattered throughout our site. It means that being an Armchair Millionaire is not about having a million dollars, but having the attitude that will get you there. It is a state of mind, rather than a number in a bank account. When you are an Armchair Millionaire, you are mindful of the future, walking on a path toward an attainable goal of financial freedom.

You'll discover as you read this book and meet actual members of our community that Armchair Millionaires come from all sorts of backgrounds. They are in different stages of life, and their portfolios are of widely varying sizes.

But there are some distinct characteristics that all Armchair Millionaires share. Once you understand these traits and begin to adopt them for yourself, you too will become an Armchair Millionaire. Even those of you who are terrified to start digging around in your personal finances. And those of you who don't think you have enough time to actually maintain an investing plan. And all the folks who dare to dream of being financially secure but don't have the first idea how to go about it—especially you!

An Armchair Millionaire Is...

Someone with a Goal

The basic goal for every Armchair Millionaire is financial security. Even though there are an infinite number of ways to define "security," we can probably all agree on this basic definition: Security is having more than you need to survive; not living paycheck to paycheck; and not lying in bed at night worrying what would happen if you lost your job or got sick.

On the other hand, having more than you need to survive doesn't necessarily mean having the best of everything—such as shaved mink coats and multiple luxury cars and adorable little six-bedroom summer cottages. If your goal is to live extravagantly, you're missing the Armchair Millionaire mantra. Money is our friend, but it's not our savior. And the less we spend, the more we'll have. Even fabulously wealthy people can spend themselves into the poorhouse. An Armchair Millionaire is too smart to do that. Which brings us to our next characteristic:

Someone with Common Sense

An Armchair Millionaire is a skeptic. Not a cynic, mind you, but a skeptic—someone who likes to know the facts before jumping to any conclusions. And someone who knows there probably aren't any quick and easy fortunes headed our way. Armchair Millionaires know the idea of getting rich quickly is a waste of our time. For that reason, we probably won't be spending our hard-earned money on lottery tickets. (Not unless the prize is really big.)

But Armchair Millionaires know that it is possible, and even likely, to get rich slowly.

One quick look at the growth of a single dollar at a 10 percent annual rate of return over two centuries ($190 million!) will show us that time and compounded returns—as you'll learn in Step 5—are very powerful tools for making a lot of money. More powerful tools than expensive brokers, or elaborate investment theories. In other words, an Armchair Millionaire is . . .

A Do-It-Yourselfer

After all, how else are you going to know that your investment plan is being done right? Sure, we'd love to have it done for us, but when it comes to the really important things, it's worth knowing how to do it ourselves—especially if we are going to rely on it.

There's another advantage to running your own plan. One of the most common investing mistakes, so common that it's legendary in investing circles, "is selling into a panic." Everyone's heard a story (or has one of their own) in which someone sold their stocks or mutual funds when the market was in a downward spiral—only to see the market quickly rebound.

When you understand how your investing plan works and how the stock market has worked historically, then you'll understand why selling into a panic is irrational. Armchair Millionaires know how their investing plans work. And they never invest in anything they aren't comfortable with.

By bringing the control over your financial freedom into your own hands, you achieve ultimate security. It's captured best in the old saying, "Give a man a portfolio and he'll invest for a day. Teach a man to invest and he'll eventually become a millionaire." (Okay, so maybe the saying doesn't go *exactly* like that, but you get the drift.)

Someone with a Plan

There isn't an Armchair Millionaire out there without a saving and investing plan that's intended to build their wealth over the long term. That's a given. But what really sets an Armchair Millionaire apart from other investors is that an Armchair Millionaire's plan can run on autopilot. The plan requires some planning, a little implementation, and then basically you never have to think about it again. Of course, if your personal style is to spend time researching investments and plotting your course, you can do so. But an Armchair Millionaire's plan works reliably and on its own while you sleep, when you're on vacation—all the time. You don't ever have to break a sweat. Just sit back and relax. Once you master the basic skills and disciplines—emotional and intellectual—that you need to build wealth, then you can use the twin levers of short-term desires vs. long-term gains to build your portfolio at any pace you want. So every Armchair Millionaire is . . .

Someone with a Portfolio

There's one last thing that any Armchair Millionaire will eventually have. It's the inevitable result of a lifetime investing program: a seven-figure portfolio.

What an Armchair Millionaire Is Not

Okay, so now you know more about what an Armchair Millionaire is. Here's a brief rundown on the things an Armchair Millionaire is not:

One thing that all Armchair Millionaires are not is perfect. When we asked our community members if they live below their means, only half said they do. If you're thinking that you lack the discipline to become an Armchair Millionaire, think again. Just starting to sort out your financial life is enough to designate you an Armchair Millionaire.

Armchair Millionaire Member Poll
Do you live below your means?
50% yes   30% no   20% sometimes

A Cheapskate

Yes, it's true that the less money you spend, the more money you'll have. But that doesn't mean you have to deny yourself anything that could be construed as a luxury. After all, it isn't unreasonable to want to enjoy the well-deserved fruits of your labors. Modern life is demanding and we all deserve to pamper ourselves now and again. What you'll learn as you develop your plan is that you can create a personalized balance between short-term desires—such as the desire for an expensive cup of coffee, or a cushy new couch—and long-term goals, such as financial freedom. This balance will decide how fast your portfolio will grow. So you can still be an Armchair Millionaire and spend money on nonessential items; you'll just take a little longer to reach your goal. The choice is entirely up to you. If you're deep in debt as you read this, your story may be a little different—but we'll cover that shortly.

An Extravagant Spender

When you hear the word *millionaire,* chances are you imagine someone with deep pockets, eating fancy dinners, ordering custom-made shirts, and flying on the Concorde for dinner in Paris. In other words, someone who never worries about money.

This image of a millionaire is so firmly entrenched in American mythology that it's hard to shake. But as we've said before, even millionaires can spend their way into the poorhouse. The first way to become an Armchair Millionaire is to curb your frivolous spending. But before you panic and say you'll never be able to do it, please finish reading this book. The Armchair Millionaire Five Steps to Financial Freedom can help you overcome your preconceived notions about money and build a commonsense savings plan that will make you rich. In other words, you'll learn how to make money work for you, not against you.

"The most popular watch among millionaires is a Seiko, a fine timepiece, moderately priced. This is also the most popular brand among CEOs of Fortune 500 companies."

—From *The Millionaire Next Door*

Bet you were expecting a Rolex, weren't you?

Someone with a Perfect Credit Report

Many Armchair Millionaires were once in debt. And they never want to be there again. Some have never been in debt, because the idea of owing just isn't for them. Still others are digging themselves out of the hole one bill at a time. As far as being an Armchair Millionaire is concerned, where you are when you start isn't important—it's where you're headed that matters.

The real beauty of the Armchair Millionaire's plan to help you achieve financial freedom is that it can work for anyone. So take a deep breath and repeat after us: "I'm ready to be a millionaire!" And turn to the next chapter. . . .

CHAPTER 2

Financial Freedom Can Be Yours

What Have You Heard in the Past About Making Money?

When you close your eyes and imagine what a successful investor looks like, what do you see? A man in a business suit chomping a cigar behind an impressive desk? A frenzied person on the floor of a stock exchange, motioning wildly and screaming "Buy!"? A genteel woman going about her daily business while her broker handles all her financial affairs behind the scenes?

There are many preconceived notions associated with investing. Mainly, that you have to be classy, smart, and wealthy, and either have a lot of time to monitor your portfolio constantly, or a near-genius broker to do all your legwork for you.

Would you believe that none of these notions is even the slightest bit true?

Wall Street is shrouded in myth and secrecy. It can seem that the only way you'll make money is if you've got "insider information" or a "hot tip." Well, friends, huddle up and get ready to hear a white-hot tip about making it in the market: You can be a complete schlub, never get out of your jammies, and still rake in the money. You can have only $100 a month to invest. You can be completely ignorant about complicated investment theories. You can be stranded on a desert island. But the point is, you (yes, you!) can achieve all your financial dreams.

Want to see what a successful investor looks like? Try picking up a mirror.

There are any number of ways you can rationalize to yourself that investing just isn't for you. But the fact is, no one else cares as much about your financial security as you do. So no one is better suited to make it happen than you are. Because if you don't take care of your own portfolio, chances are you won't have one. There's no need to panic. You can do this.

The fact of the matter is, investing and personal finance are rarely explained and taught in the real world—not in schools, not at the family dinner table, and certainly not among friends. This lack of discussion creates a situation in which the average person assumes that investing must be so difficult that it is out of his or her reach. Here, two Armchair Millionaire members talk about investing ignorance and how to get over it.

Are We Pathetic?

Q: "My husband and I are, I think, educated, intelligent people, except when it comes to money. We have close to $50,000 in a checking account, because we don't know what to do with it, or how, so we just leave it there. I am almost ashamed to admit this—who on earth doesn't know how to invest money? Is this a common problem, or so pathetic it doesn't warrant a reply?"

—Armchair Millionaire member Judi33

Start with a Change in Perception

A: "Investing money is like any other skill—it has to be learned. Many of us find that while we are growing up, money is presented to us as a substitute or symbol for all kinds of things, especially personal worth. We are made to feel guilty or greedy if we pay too much attention to it, and too stupid to understand all the complexities of managing it if we don't [pay enough attention to it]. In reality, money is a tool to express our values and what we want to do with our lives. Once you realize that, then all the rest of this starts to make sense. Congratulations on getting started."

—Armchair Millionaire member Jones_Ch

What You Will Learn in This Book

The best thing you could do to start your new life as an investor is to take all the ideas you have about investing and throw them right out the window. What you'll come to understand as you read this book is that investing is not only easy, it's boring. Kind of like brushing your teeth. Once you figured out how to brush your teeth, you never thought much about it again, did you? But you still brush every day, right? (If you answered "No," that's okay—your Armchair Millionaire portfolio will grow even on those days when you don't brush your teeth.)

MEET RICH

Rich is the official mascot of ArmchairMillionaire.com on the World Wide Web. Don't let appearances deceive you, though—Rich is much more than just a two-dimensional cartoon character. Throughout this book (as well as on ArmchairMillionaire.com), you'll occasionally find Rich explaining basic concepts of personal finance. He'll help to describe some of the strategies that lie behind the Armchair Millionaire philosophy. Above all, Rich is here to remind you that saving and investing don't have to be complicated.

So how is it possible that everything you've learned about the stock market is wrong? The Armchair Millionaire Five Steps to Financial Freedom are designed to alleviate all your worries about investing as well as help you build a seven-figure portfolio. Here are some of the mondo-sized myths that Armchair Millionaires tell us they used to hold to be true, lock, stock, and barrel (before they saw the light, of course).

BIG MYTH NO. 1:
You have to have money to make money.

REALITY CHECK: Well, of course you have to start with some amount of money. But it's never too early to start saving, even if it's $25 per paycheck. The thing about money you invest is that it grows. Over time, it begins to grow upon itself so no matter how much you start with, you're going to end up with a lot more.

Sure, there are lots of planners who won't accept a client unless she has thousands and thousands of dollars. Many brokerage firms require an initial minimum investment of $1,000 or more. Some mutual funds make you invest up to $10,000 or more in order to open an account!

But just because some companies cater to people who already have money doesn't mean that they all do. In fact, you can start your saving and investing plan with less than the cost of this book. There are mutual funds that will accept an initial investment of $25 or less. There are brokers with whom you can open an account with no minimum investment. (For a complete list of such funds and brokers, refer to the Appendices B and C.) Armchair Millionaires know that it doesn't require a fortune to get started investing. When you make yourself a priority, it's just a matter of time.

BIG MYTH NO. 2:

You have to have a lot of time to invest wisely.

REALITY CHECK: Once you've set up your portfolio—a process we'll cover soon enough—*you don't have to do anything else.* Except watch your money grow. Instead of sweating over stock reports, take up a fulfilling hobby. Knowing that you've got your finances in order is probably going to give you a greater sense of well-being, and you're going to need an outlet to let all those good feelings flow. Catch up on all the letters you've meant to write but haven't. Volunteer some time at the hospital, or learn to tap dance.

Of course, if you're in need of a hobby, then learning how to analyze stocks might be a good one. Most hobbies can end up costing you a bundle, but investing in stocks is a hobby that can potentially make you money. But this book isn't about that—we're only going to cover how to build your core portfolio using the Armchair Millionaire's approach to investing. Researching and investing in individual stocks would be a separate piece of your overall investment strategy, and entirely optional.

When you invest as an Armchair Millionaire, time actually becomes your friend, allowing your money to grow exponentially. We'll talk more about that in Chapter 9, "Start Today—Put the Power of Compound Interest to Work for You."

BIG MYTH NO. 3:

You need a degree in business, or you must be a math whiz, or you should be able to understand complicated formulas in order to be a successful investor.

REALITY CHECK: While we said that you could become an Armchair Millionaire without the aid of a professional, it's also true that you don't need any special knowledge of math or business. You won't need any of the algebra you've forgotten since high school. You won't need to take accounting classes at night, or even know how to use a computer if you don't want to (although we believe this book will make a case for how using a computer to tap into a community of like-minded investors can enhance your investing experience).

A friend of ours likes to tell a story about how he nearly didn't graduate from high school because of a mishap in calculus class. Two terms of failing grades meant that he needed to pass the final in order to pass the class, and he needed to pass the class in order to have enough credits to graduate. On the final, he achieved a D⁻ (whether through study, luck, or the teacher's sympathy he'll never know) and proceeded to graduate on schedule.

His bad math experience behind him, our friend successfully completed a liberal arts education, and never took another mathematics course in his four years of college. He embarked on a career in the performing arts, and later took up investing for his retirement and to support his growing family. And you know what? His math-phobia hasn't impeded his investing success whatsoever. His portfolio continues to chug right along—because he invests sensibly as an Armchair Millionaire, and not strictly by the numbers.

Contrary to popular belief, complexity is not a necessary component of a financial plan. Once you understand how the market works—and you will, after you read Chapter 8, "Use the Armchair Investing Strategy"—you'll see that the simplest investment plans are best. So you can earn just as high a rate of return as the most famous investment gurus. And you don't have to pay anyone else to make your portfolio decisions for you.

BIG MYTH NO. 4:

Once you hit it big in the markets, you will have a wonderful, extravagant life and nothing bad will ever happen to you again.

REALITY CHECK: Financial security is a beautiful thing, but it's not going to make you a fairy princess or a movie star. You will achieve financial security through common sense and a serious—though low-maintenance—commitment to financial responsibility. If, once you achieve the portfolio of your dreams, you forget about common sense and commitment and start spending money willy-nilly, you will lose it. Money can help us live the lives we want to lead, but it can't fix all of our problems.

BIG MYTH NO. 5:

It's too hard to figure out how the stock market works.

REALITY CHECK: The stock market in the United States is actually older than our country itself. The New York Stock Exchange, the largest stock exchange in the world, began in downtown Manhattan in the early 1700s when a bunch of guys stood around on a street corner buying and selling pieces of paper. These pages represented shares in companies, and the price of each share was set by negotiation between the buyer and the seller. Pretty simple!

Believe it or not, the stock market today works exactly the same way. Of course, today we have brokers and computers and big investment banks who buy and sell millions of shares each day, but the price of each trade is determined by the negotiation between the buyer and the seller. Sure, you could delve into the details of how the market works, from the operations of an auction exchange to learning the intricate hand signals used by traders on the trading floor. But just as you don't need to be trained as a gourmet chef in order to appreciate a fabulous meal at a four-star restaurant, understanding the intricacies of the stock market isn't a prerequisite for becoming a successful investor.

In fact, the single most important thing you need to know about the stock market can be summed up in a few words: It goes up over the long term. In the history of the modern stock market, it's easy to see that the market goes up in seven out of every ten years. Sure, it goes down, too—the market has declined 10 percent or more fifty-three times since 1900. You can expect the stock market to see a drop of 10 percent or more every two years, on average. And the market has seen declines greater than 25 percent fifteen times in the past one hundred years, or an average of once every six years.

But here's the key: The market has a 100 percent success rate in bouncing back every single time it has fallen—if you just give it enough time. With odds like those, what more do you need to know about how the market works?

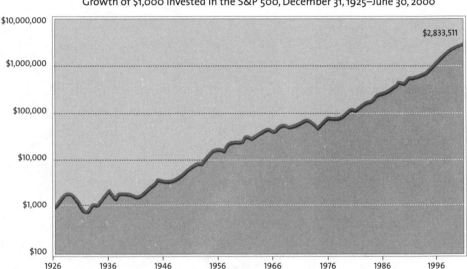

Growth of $1,000 Invested in the S&P 500, December 31, 1925–June 30, 2000

BIG MYTH NO. 6:

If you want to be a successful investor, you have to stay on top of the market each day.

REALITY CHECK: Chances are that you can turn on the television right now and have your choice of several financial television programs or entire channels devoted to money. There are thousands of Web sites devoted to the topic of investing. In New York City, there's even a radio station that exclusively broadcasts business and investing news twenty-four hours a day. It's easy to succumb to the belief that you *need* to be on top of every blip in the market, that you can't afford to miss any piece of news that might affect your portfolio.

We believe that the information revolution has brought great things to our world. You can tune in to TV stations, radio programs, and Web sites from all over the world, and learn new things and be introduced to new cultures. Unfortunately, the sheer amount of information that's constantly bombarding us presents another problem: How do we figure out what's important when we try to take in all this information?

There's a term that Armchair Millionaires use when describing information overload: "noise." Nearly all of the "news" that we hear on a daily basis is absolutely useless in managing a sensible long-term financial plan. And investors who listen to this noise and try to react quickly will nearly always find that they lose out. There are hyperactive traders, including day traders, who are equipped to profit from all the bouncing around the stock market may do in the short term. Day traders try to capitalize on ultra-short-term gyrations in the market by making big bets on where a stock is headed in the next few minutes. It's fruitless for most individual investors to try to focus on active trading strategies such as these, for a couple of reasons. Most of us just can't spend hours a day glued to our computer monitors—we have jobs to do! And taxes and commissions take away big chunks of any profits that you might make as a hyperactive trader.

The Armchair Millionaire's plan for financial success doesn't require you to pay any attention whatsoever to the daily influx of "news" and information you may hear or read about the markets. You can safely ignore your portfolio for months and still be successful! In these busy times, don't you have better things to do than try to outfox the pros? Especially when the odds are stacked against you if you do try.

BIG MYTH NO. 7:
You're better off working with a stockbroker or financial advisor than trying to invest yourself.

REALITY CHECK: Let's just get this out of the way right now: There are plenty of people who can benefit from the services of a smart and sensible broker or financial advisor. If you've got lots and lots of money, or have a lot of your net worth tied up in your own business, or have some other particularly complicated financial situation, then you should find a good financial planner—and pronto. Planners often provide important services such as tax planning, estate planning, and life insurance evaluations, and the good ones can even help you build a portfolio that's profitable.

But one of the financial industry's dirty little secrets is that most pros can't even beat the market averages, so don't expect your broker to have the inside track to investing success. There's a classic investing book from the 1930s, *Where Are the Customers' Yachts?*, that takes its title from a visit the book's author made to a Manhattan yacht club with the president of an investment firm. The esteemed financier was pointing out all the yachts that belonged to partners in the firm, obvious symbols of their success. The young author's response upon seeing these expensive toys was, "Where are the customers' yachts?" This is a not-so-subtle reminder that financial professionals don't necessarily generate their personal wealth from their investing prowess, but from what they're paid by their clients.

If you're the type of person who tries to fix the leak yourself before calling the plumber, then you can be a successful investor *without* a broker. You'll be no better or worse off than someone in your same situation who hired a planner—and chances are good that you'll come out ahead since you'll save on fees and commissions.

The Armchair Millionaire's financial freedom plan is one that you can implement all by yourself, without professional assistance.

BIG MYTH NO. 8:

Rich people are the only people who have the connections and the resources needed to invest successfully in the stock market.

REALITY CHECK: One Armchair Millionaire member, Candis K., said it best: "The market doesn't care about the color of my skin, my ethnic background, my weight, my clothes, how much money I have, or whether I even have a college or high school degree." Here's a little mathematics quiz to prove the point (yeah, we know we said you wouldn't have to know much math, but don't worry, this isn't too hard):

> Which investor had a greater return—the one who invested $1,000,000 and made a profit of $100,000, or the one who invested $100 and made a profit of $15?

Sure, $100,000 is a heckuva lot bigger than $15, but that $100,000 is only a 10 percent return on the million-dollar investment. On the other hand, $15 is a 15 percent return on an investment of $100. That's 50 percent better than the million-dollar investor did. In dollar terms, there's a big difference, but in percentage terms, the smaller investor did better.

So, don't worry about the size of your portfolio, or how much you can afford to invest. You don't have to be a millionaire to invest like one, and chances are you'll eventually end up a millionaire yourself if you follow our advice. Remember, it's not how much you start out with, it's how much you end up with.

BIG MYTH NO. 9:
Saving money is too hard.

REALITY CHECK: Lots of things in life are hard. Climbing Mount Everest is hard. Programming a VCR is hard. Saving money, though, *isn't* hard—once you know the secret.

So what's the secret? Too many people think of savings as what's left over after you pay for all the essentials in life—things like food, drink, clothes, and shelter. The truth is, budgeting is nearly impossible to do successfully—if you wait until you've paid all your expenses to save money, chances are there won't be any cash left to save. Every month, unexpected expenses can arise, whether it's new tires or a shoe sale. And then, poof! Your budget is shot.

Later on in this book, you'll find out how to start a savings plan that takes care of itself once and for all just as soon as you get it started. It comes down to this: Stop thinking about ways to build your net worth, and just get started.

BIG MYTH NO. 10:

Since the stock market can crash at any time, it's best to avoid it altogether.

REALITY CHECK: There are two truths about the stock market: It goes down and it goes up. Sometimes it booms, and sometimes it crashes. But see BIG MYTH NO. 5—the market *always* recovers, over time.

This simple bit of knowledge can fortify you to withstand any downturns as long as you have time as your ally. If you don't have five years or more until you need the money that you've invested, then you'll take other measures, including keeping some of your money out of the market. But for long-term investing, you simply can't beat the stock market.

People who avoid the stock market for this reason have a big misunderstanding about how "risk" and "reward" work when it comes to investing. Any time you invest, even if it's in a bank savings account, you put your money at risk. But the good thing about risk is that as you increase the risk you're willing to take on, you have the potential to receive better returns on your investment.

Academic researchers have discovered that in order to obtain the highest rate of return on your portfolio, you need to be invested in the stock market. And if you have the power of time on your side, you can invest 100 percent of your portfolio in stocks. A portfolio that only includes stocks may go up and down in value more than a portfolio that might include bonds and/or cash, but over the long term it grows more and faster than other assets, such as bonds, CDs, or real estate. If you want to become an Armchair Millionaire, you need to invest in the stock market. Period.

BIG MYTH NO. 11:
You can make lots of money fast in the stock market—if you know the secrets.

REALITY CHECK: Thomas O'Hara, Chairman of the National Association of Investors Corp. (NAIC), a leading investor education group in the United States, likes to say that "if there was a secret way to quickly achieve wealth, wouldn't someone have figured it out by now and wouldn't the U.S. be a country of millionaires?"

The truth is, the biggest secret about the stock market is that there are no secrets. There's nothing new about the Armchair Millionaire's plan to help you achieve financial freedom—no previously undisclosed strategy or recent academic discovery that's changed the world of finance. In fact, many professional financial advisors and institutional investors use the Armchair Millionaire approach to investing. But no one has brought together all of these steps in such a sensible, easy-to-implement way. Until now.

It is possible for the average person to get a grip on their finances. And the best part is, you don't have to do it alone. There are thousands of other Armchair Millionaires who are making their financial security a reality, one year at a time.

The Gallery of Armchair Millionaires
Meet Candis—Suburban Housewife and Investor Extraordinaire

Get ready to meet a real live member of the Armchair Millionaire community. She didn't know much about investing when she started out. She had been discouraged by brokers. But now she's right on track to retire in fifteen years.

Armchair Millionaire Member Name: Candis

From: Michigan

Age: 46

Occupation: Queen of Domestic Chaos, Liege of the Laundry Room, Kid Wrangler. (I used to be in sales, I now teach National Association of Investors stock selection classes on a volunteer basis through the local adult education program.)

Family Status: Married with two children

Financial Goals: To be able to retire (extremely, very, lazily) comfortably in fifteen years or fewer. I also want to be able to afford to send my boys to Harvard if they choose to go.

What got you started investing?

I became disgusted and frustrated with:

1. The lousy rate of interest from passbook savings.
2. The lousy advice and treatment I received from a stockbroker when I was in my twenties and wanted to invest $700. He said, and I quote, "You don't have enough money to invest." This was around 1975. If I had invested that $700 in stocks then . . . twenty-two years later . . . *sigh*.
3. After some experiences I had, in addition to those mentioned above, I realized that stockbrokers were not my friends, no matter how much I paid them, and that I had best just learn how to invest because no one cared more about my future than I did.

What were your misconceptions about investing before you started?

That I had to stay glued to the television or ticker tape to be able to make a profit in the market. I remember when I was pregnant with my first child and I was learning, really learning, about the market at the same time; I would sit on the couch and watch the ticker tape on the telly for hours on end, convinced that an eighth or a quarter of a point would make a big difference in my financial future twenty years hence. Of course the fact that I was pregnant, full of those wonderful things called pregnancy hormones, didn't help the clarity of my thought a great deal.

Biggest investment blunder you've made?
Selling Sun Microsystems after I had tripled my money in it. That was two splits ago. I paid $3,900 for it less than ten years ago. I sold it for $12,000. It would be worth $84,000 now had I kept it. (Sob, sob, sob, sob, boo hoo!)

What did you learn from this blunder?
Never, and I mean never, sell a stock if the fundamentals say "hold." I listened to the talking heads on the television nattering on about doomsday scenarios for the stock. Trust yourself—look at the fundamentals of the company and if the talking heads say "sell," don't sell the stock, buy more.

What do you want the world to know about investing?
You can do it! It is not rocket science. Heck, you just need to be able to do fifth grade math, and if you can afford a cheap calculator, you don't even need to know how to do the math. You just need to be able to listen with both ears, study with both eyes, and use your one brain. If you can follow a cookie recipe, you have all the skills you need to invest in the stock market successfully.

Get Ready for a Fantastic Voyage

You have a great journey ahead of you on the road to financial freedom. Some of it will be hard, but for the most part, it's ridiculously easy. And with just a small amount of determination and open-mindedness, the hard parts won't be hard at all.

Just as with any new undertaking—such as, say, learning to ski—the first few steps toward implementing a financial plan can be scary.

The first time you take a little chunk of your paycheck and stash it away in an investing account, it might seem like there's no way you'll make it to the next payday.

The emphasis on that last sentence is on the word *seem,* because once you make it to that next payday, you'll realize that "paying yourself first" is not only good for you, it's relatively painless and richly rewarding.

Getting your financial plan in motion may be two of the hardest things you've ever done on a voluntary basis. But once you get started, it's all downhill from there (and that goes for skiing too!). Imagine the day, a year from now, when you check the balance in your investment account and see that your money has grown without any mental anguish or effort on your part. You'll find that you are well on your way to making a down payment on a house, sending your kids to college, or financing that trip around the world you've always fantasized about.

Can't you just see yourself in a beautiful home, with a lot of money in the bank? (Or insert your own goal here.) Just by reading this book, you're already on your way.

ADVICE FROM RICH

It doesn't pay to put off starting your saving and investing plan, even for only one year. If you start today and invest $100 a month in a portfolio that gives you an average return of 10 percent a year, you'll have $72,399 in twenty years, tripling your total investment of $24,000.

However, if you put off starting for another five years, and then invest $100 a month for fifteen years, you'll end up with just $40,162, a bit more than double your total investment of $18,000. It doesn't take a math whiz to see that ending up with $72,399 (three times your initial investment) is more attractive—a lot more attractive—than just barely doubling your investment and ending up with $40,162.

But what if you wait until one year from now to start your plan? In nineteen years, you'd have $64,668. Not too shabby, but significantly less than $72,399. To be exact, the penalty for waiting one year turns out to be $6,531. When was the last time you turned down a gift of $6,531?

Chapter 2 Action Items

Before you start your full-fledged plan, it's important to make sure what your goals are. This chapter should help you see that financial freedom is possible. Chapter 3 can help you get your head and heart straight to define those goals, and to give you the wherewithal to achieve them.

- Think about what stereotypes you associate with successful investors. Then forget them.
- Read Chapter 3.

Preparing Your Head and Heart for Achieving Financial Success

Are you ready—really ready—to become a millionaire? You can have all the knowledge in the world about investing, but if you don't have the right frame of mind for success, you're likely to end up making the same mistakes over and over again.

Let's face it—resolving to invest for your future is one of the most "grown-up" decisions you'll ever make, no matter how old or young you are. In the face of all the conflicting information you may see and hear from friends and colleagues, in the media, and even from financial professionals, you might feel like you're back in grade school trying to learn how to write letter *E*'s that aren't backward.

One of the reasons that investing seems like such a "grown-up" activity is that you have to be eighteen years old before you can legally own stocks or mutual funds (you can start investing before that age, you'll just need a custodian to oversee your account). Add this to the list of life's little ironies: You can legally drive a one-ton mass of steel, aluminum, chrome, and rubber at 65 miles an hour down an interstate highway years before you can legally own a share of stock.

But the real reason investing is a grown-up decision is because it means assessing your goals, analyzing your current status, and formulating a plan that will turn your goals into a reality. You're going to have to use both parts of your brain—the rational half to determine your steps, and the emotional half to give yourself the resolve to take those steps. This is not necessarily hard to do, but it is big. Not quite as big as having a baby, but definitely bigger than switching long-distance carriers.

What will have to happen in order to make you fully committed to starting an investment plan? It varies from person to person. For one Armchair Millionaire, sitting down to define her goals with her husband helped her see the light. For another, it took tracking every little expense to see exactly where her money was going. Here and on the next pages, Armchair Millionaires talk about what gives them the resolve they need to take control of their financial lives.

We are going to do it!

"My husband and I together have over $50,000 in debt. We both make relatively good money, but the burden of these debts is almost unbearable. We sat down last night and really assessed our goals. We want to be homeowners. We want enough land to have a healthy garden. We want dogs and cats. We want to be able to live on one income when we decide to have little ones. We want to travel before we have these kids. All of this takes patience and saving and good habits.

"We are learning now, at a young age, that anything worth having requires patience and saving. So often we buy things to appease our urges for instant gratification. It feels good for a few minutes, but then the weight of knowing that money could be better spent paying off a card or going into a savings account sinks in. Ugh. That is an awful feeling."

—Armchair Millionaire member ali_w

Armchair Millionaires realize that they can bring together both sides of their brains into the process of carrying out a sensible saving and investing plan. They let their dreams and goals empower their path to success (as defined by having an investment plan that provides them with more money than they need to survive), tempered with realism and a good dose of skepticism.

If It Isn't Hard, Why Doesn't Everyone Invest?

Investing seems intimidating until you've done it the first time. Many people get nervous about the prospect of buying their first car or house, applying for that first mortgage or car loan, filing their first tax return, getting their first job. After the initial haze of the experience clears, they have a better idea of what to expect the next time.

But unlike tax returns and mortgages, investing doesn't have a deadline, making it seem easy to put off. How many times have you said, "Next year, I'm really going to get my finances in order"? But the sooner you invest, the more time your money has to grow. Starting today versus starting next year can have a big impact on your future financial situation.

But before you start thinking that you've already waited too long and all hope is lost, remember that whenever you set out toward financial freedom for the first time, your age doesn't matter. You could be a thirty-year-old entrepreneur, a twenty-two-year-old college grad, or a sixty-five-year-old retiree—the decision to work toward financial freedom means taking personal responsibility. It means taking positive action to meet your goals. It means acting like a "grown-up."

Once you get going, it's important that you are comfortable with your investment plan. If you wake up in the middle of the night in a cold sweat because you're worried about your portfolio, you've got a problem. If you're biting your fingernails to the quick because you're worried that you might be missing out on the stock market's big moves, you've also got a problem. The trouble may be with your plan, or it may be that you're just not clear about your financial goals and how you'll reach them. Either way, you need to get intimate with your investing plan. Take the time to snuggle up with your portfolio. Unburden all your personal secrets. Become good friends. Because if you're not 100 percent satisfied with your personal financial plan, it just isn't going to work.

ADVICE FROM RICH

Don't confuse skepticism with cynicism. It's good to use a bit of restraint and caution when it comes to investing. When we were kids, we were taught never to jump into a lake or swimming pool until we knew how deep or shallow the water was, and what might be lurking beneath the surface. Likewise, you should never, ever invest in anything that you don't understand until you know all the risks and the potential rewards and the most likely outcome.

Investing is a lot like an important relationship. Your investing plan and your relationships will both work only if you're willing to stick together through ups and downs, for better and for worse. It's only natural that you may get emotional at times, or that you'll make a stupid mistake, or get caught doing something you shouldn't have done—whether it's forgetting to take out the trash or taking a flier on an IPO you hear about from some broker who calls you up while you're eating dinner. That's when you'll kiss and make up, and move on. It's the grown-up thing to do.

If only it were that easy to separate your emotional attachment to money from what you *know* in your mind is the right thing to do. Unfortunately, we're all human, so it's unreasonable to expect us to act like investing robots. You might misjudge your tolerance for the occasional ups and downs of a portfolio, and react to short-term news when you should be holding on to a long-term vision—even if you know the truth that comes from looking at the facts. Coming to terms with your own ability to make mistakes requires a great deal of maturity. The better you know yourself and your own bad habits, the more successful you'll be.

So, are you ready for a system of saving and investing that:

- Is easy to implement?
- Is easy to understand?
- Makes sense to you?
- Empowers you?
- And best of all, will make you rich?

Then read on!

Regaining Control of My Money!

"I can identify with anyone who has a feeling of desperation about their finances. I was in the same boat until a friend advised that I take control of my money and gave me some hints on how to begin. The first thing I needed to do was to see, on paper, how much money was coming in versus how much was going out, and then to track down where any unaccounted-for money was going. These two steps were real eye-openers for me! The first revelation was that I definitely didn't need to be as broke as I was. By beginning to write down every little expense, I have begun to see where the extra spending has caused so many problems for me. Another benefit of writing down each penny spent is that it makes me think twice about spending it—do I really need that magazine just because Brad Pitt is on the cover of it?! From here I hope to establish a firm budget that will help me save for my retirement and my kids' college educations. I had thought that it was too late for either of those things, but now, with a plan in front of me I can see that it can be done."

—Armchair Millionaire member jujubee71

Beginning Your Journey

You wouldn't get into your car and drive across the country on your summer vacation unless you had mastered a few basic skills and had a good idea of where you were going and how you'd get there. For instance, before you back out of the driveway, you need to know:

1. How to drive a car. You don't need to know how a four-stroke engine works, but to be a successful driver you do need to know how to steer, brake, accelerate, and turn.
2. Where you are headed. If you don't know where you're going when you start your trip, you'll never get there—it's guaranteed!
3. How you'll get there. A good road map is essential for a cross-country car trip. You even might map out your route with a high-lighter before getting started. Or you might start off with a general sense of how to get to your destination, knowing that you could stop and ask for directions if you really needed to (obviously, if you're a man you'd never do that, but women always see it as a viable option).

Those are the basic requirements for taking a road trip in your car. They're not so different from how you'll go about building your savings and investing plan.

1. You don't need to understand how the stock market works in its most mundane details in order to profit from investing in stocks.
2. You do need to identify the reasons or goals that you're working toward. It could be that you're saving for retirement or college for the kids or a summer home or a boat or to start a business or even to allow you to retire at forty-five. Defining a goal not only gives you something to shoot for, it also determines how much time you have to get there. If you don't have a goal, or if your goal is something vague like "I want to be rich" or "I want to make money fast," chances are you'll never get there.

Some people keep a postcard from a tropical island, or a photo of their dream home tacked up on their refrigerator or bulletin board, just to help keep a mental picture of the goals they're working toward.

3. You need a plan to get you toward your goals. However, you don't have to create a plan that budgets all the fun out of life. There will be detours along the way, but a sound plan will get you to your destination in time.

In order to make the right preparations to make the transformation to an Armchair Millionaire, you need to empty your brain of everything you've ever been told about investing and personal finance. You need to forget everything you've heard on television, everything you've read in financial magazines, every piece of junk mail you've seen that's tried to sell you an investing newsletter, and every Web site that's promised you the secrets to quick wealth. Forget all those infomercials and advertisements.

And while you're reading this book, ignore what your sister-in-law or fishing buddy has told you about hot stock picks. If someone tries to wow you with investing stories at a cocktail party, change the subject to pets, or the weather.

And as you read, every time you hear yourself saying "But . . . ," try keeping your mind (both sides of it) open.

The Last 10 Percent

There's an old saying that "success is 90 percent perspiration and 10 percent inspiration." You can break down successful investing in much the same way. You'll get 90 percent of the way to financial freedom using the knowledge and tools in this book. But the last 10 percent comes from the heart. And that's often the hardest part. Your own bad habits can get in the way. You'll need to stop being afraid of money, and start taking control of your own financial future.

You deserve to feel financially secure, and you are the only person who can make it happen. Don't let that nay-saying voice in your head keep you from investing. Combat that voice by listening to your heart instead.

Simple, but not EASY

"Losing weight is simple: eat less, exercise more. But many of us know, it's not easy. Only when motivation overcomes resistance do we make progress. Likewise, 'spend less, save more' is simple, but not easy. Savor the struggle that will make you stronger. Try to find others who would be interested in forming a support group. Hang in there and make your financial plan work. After all, what's the alternative?"

—Armchair Millionaire member habitatmom

Getting Ready to Be a Successful Investor

To help you start down the road toward becoming an Armchair Millionaire, here are some practical tips.

JOIN AN ONLINE INVESTMENT COMMUNITY, SUCH AS THE ARMCHAIR MILLIONAIRE. There is strength in numbers. On the Armchair Millionaire Web site (http://www.armchairmillionaire.com), you can meet many of the investors profiled in this book, as well as others who are on their own journeys to financial freedom. Chances are that you will meet someone who's in the same place in their life right now as you are, or someone who's been there already and can lend a helping hand. Best of all, everything at the Armchair Millionaire is free.

JOIN OR FORM AN INVESTMENT CLUB. Many investors find that investment clubs are a great way to learn about investing, as well as to invest in the stock market. You could even start one with a few friends and get the support you need to further your investment education.

For more information about investment clubs, contact the National Association of Investors Corp. (NAIC):

NAIC
P.O. Box 220
Royal Oak, MI 48068
877-ASK-NAIC (toll-free)
248-583-NAIC
248-583-4880 (fax)
http://www.better-investing.org
service@better-investing.org

Another resource for investment clubs is a Web site called Investment Club Central. They feature a directory of investment club Web sites, as well as tutorials and articles:
http://www.iclubcentral.com.

REASSURE YOURSELF. If you don't have a computer, yet, get one! But you don't need a computer to get the reassurance you need to get started. Instead, write reassuring notes to yourself and paste them on your bathroom mirror or refrigerator or on top of your checkbook—anyplace where you'll see them regularly. Come up with a few messages that will remind you of your goals, like "I want to retire a millionaire!" or "Pay yourself—you're worth it!" Or tear out a picture of your dream house, or mountain cabin, or your alma mater (where Junior will surely want to matriculate) and tape it up as well. These reminders of your dreams and goals will inspire you to make them come true.

TAKE THE NEXT STEP. We think you're ready now to take the next step toward financial freedom, so turn to the next chapter.

Chapter 3 Action Items

- Make up your mind—the rational half and the emotional half— that financial freedom can be yours.
- Find ways to keep that resolve, either by joining an online investing community, starting an investment club, or writing yourself encouraging notes. Experiment and discover what works best for you.

CHAPTER 4

Dealing with Your Debt

Americans love to borrow money. We've racked up over a trillion dollars in consumer debt in this country, all so we can live in big houses (paid for with 20 percent down and thirty years of paying off the mortgage) and drive big cars (paid for with a four-year auto loan). We can buy anything we want, whether we can afford it or not, just by whipping out a piece of plastic and telling the cashier to "Charge it!" Have you ever seen a commercial for a credit card in which people aren't smiling, laughing, and doing fun things? It's fun to spend when it all just goes on the card!

On second thought, maybe *love* isn't the right word to describe our fatal attraction to borrowed money. Perhaps *obsession* is a better description of the "buy now, pay later" habits of Americans. There was once a time when personal bankruptcy was looked upon with scorn. Now, the stigma is gone, and more people are filing for bankruptcy than ever before. According to the American Bankruptcy Institute, a record number of people, 1,398,182, filed for personal bankruptcy in 1998—an increase of 94.7 percent since 1990. What's worse, some people have made a habit of bankruptcy, spending themselves into an enormous hole, then begging for protection from the bankruptcy courts, only to repeat the whole process all over again.

When You're in Too Deep: The Five Warning Signs
ADVICE FROM RICH

How can you tell when your debt is out of control? Answer the five questions below. If you answered "yes" to any of these questions, you may be losing the credit card battle.

- Do you only make the minimum monthly payment required on your cards?
- Is your credit limit maxed on most of your cards?
- Do you use credit cards for day-to-day purchases like groceries, movie tickets, or fast food?
- Do you use cash advances on one card to pay off another?
- Do you ever make a purchase just to earn frequent flier miles?
- Do you routinely spend more than you earn?

Sure, there's nothing like the feeling you get from whipping out a credit card and taking home that new book or CD or computer gadget. At least, that is, until the bill arrives. It's easy to shake the credit card hangover, though, by making the minimum payment and forgetting about the whole mess until next month, when another bill arrives.

The feeling of despair that comes as you charge down the credit card highway is bad enough. The deeper you fall into debt, the more helpless you feel about ever getting out.

The worst part of this vicious circle, though, is it's downright impossible to save when you're barely making the minimum payments on your credit cards each month. Many wannabe Armchair Millionaires ask "How can I start my saving and investing plan when I'm mired in debt?"

The good news is that it's not impossible. No matter how much debt you have, you *can* get out. If you're in debt over your head, it can certainly *seem* like all your financial goals are way out of reach.

But it's not impossible to reverse directions and get started on the path to financial freedom. And you don't have to be one of those 100 percent debt-free, pay-cash-for-everything superhumans, either. All you need to do is take charge of your personal debts. With the right plan, you can defeat the debt monster while building your nest egg.

How Armchair Millionaires Save and Pay Off Debts at the Same Time

One of the most frustrating things about debt is the feeling that you have to dig yourself out of the hole before you can even think about moving forward with your investing plans. But it doesn't have to work that way. Here, Armchair Millionaires explain how they've managed to do both at the same time—and what to avoid in your quest to demolish your debt.

Put Your Savings to Work

"My husband and I have a goal to pay off our credit card debt. We have opened a savings account, and every time we have $1,000 accumulated we take $500 and put it toward the credit card. (We have consolidated our debt onto one card.) The 'cushion' $500 is always there in case we have an emergency and that way we should not have to charge anything."

—Armchair Millionaire member dkdk123

What Not to Do

"We just cashed out my husband's 401(k) to pay off debts, and the taxes and penalties killed us! The debt is gone, but now so is every penny we ever saved, and a lot of it we never saw. There's usually a 10–15 percent penalty fee for taking it out before retirement on top of the taxes, so we only saw two-thirds of what was once ours."

—Armchair Millionaire member JacJ.

Of course, if you're truly the type who already pays off your credit card bills each month, and are happy with your current mortgage and auto loan, you can skip this chapter entirely. Otherwise, it's time to get motivated!

From the Armchair Millionaire's Gallery— A Look at Real People Who Really Invest

One feature of the Armchair Millionaire Web site is the Armchair Millionaire's Gallery—where you can meet real people and learn their stories and ideas about investing. Here are two excerpts from Gallery, featuring two people who were once about to tear their hair out over their debts. Not only have these folks been there, but they've managed to pull themselves out of debt and become successful investors. Before you decide there's no way you can ever demolish your debt, read on.

Up from the Depths

Armchair Millionaire Member Name: Steve J.

From: Florida

Age: 33

Occupation: Medically retired military personnel

Family Status: Married with children

Investment Goals: To enjoy a comfortable retirement and to be able to handle emergencies in the meantime.

Background: I have a chronic disease, and due to medical bills, I lost everything that I had—I even lived in my car at one point. But I have worked my way back up to a point where I'm seeing the benefits of saving and investing and will continue until I reach my goal! My wife and I always used to spend all of our money, until we started having money automatically deducted from our checking account and added to our investment account. It took me a long time to get smart about money because I was always trying to keep up with my neighbors in having the newest, most expensive of everything. I spent it all. Now my wife and I discuss our investments for all of our goals. We do it as a team. We just didn't realize that a little financial planning goes a long way. Now I'm teaching my kids to start saving every month, and how to compare prices, and shop clearance.

Just Starting Out

Armchair Millionaire Member Name: Nondas S.

From: New York

Age: 32

Occupation: Administrative assistant

Family Status: Divorced

Investment Goals: To pay for son's college education, stay out of debt, and have money to retire.

Background: No one in my family saves. They are into buying the most expensive clothes and jewelry. I used to have huge credit card bills, then I lost my job and couldn't pay any creditors, much less put savings in the bank. I thought because I had so little money I couldn't start my financial plan. Now I go to the 99-cent stores and always buy things on sale. I contribute to my 401(k) at work and my company matches the funds and now I take $1,000 a month and put it in savings to invest. I have only started to work toward my goals, and I wish I had more time to follow my portfolio. But I am on the right track, and that feels good.

Putting Your "Defeat Your Debt" Plan into Place

One piece of advice that's often given to debt-laden investors is to pay down *all* your debts before you start saving. The rationale for this bit of wisdom is that paying off a credit card that charges you an interest rate of 18 percent is like getting a guaranteed rate of return of 18 percent on your money. That's a better return than you'll get on just about any investment.

It sure sounds like a good deal. But the success of this approach depends on a complete and total change of your money behavior patterns. If you could eliminate your bad habits that quickly, you probably wouldn't be in such bad shape in the first place!

The Armchair Millionaire approach to paying down your debt is both practical and effective. You can put your plan into effect using our arsenal of five "Debt Busters." They'll take some work (and some time), but the rewards will be more than worth it. By sticking to the plan, you *will* become debt free, and you will get your saving and investing plan started, as well.

DEBT BUSTER #1: KNOW YOUR ENEMY. Before you begin the battle, you have to know what you're up against. And that means getting intimate with your credit cards, loans, and any other debts.

How much do you really know about your debts? Without looking, can you name all the credit cards in your wallet or pocketbook, and the interest rate each one charges? Do you know the balances you're carrying from month to month? And do you even know what a "grace period" is, not to mention how long it is for each of your credit cards? How much of your auto loan payment goes to interest and how much actually pays for your car?

It's pretty easy to get to know more about all your debts. All you need to do is make a list. You can use the worksheet in the sidebar on pages 44–45 to help you get organized.

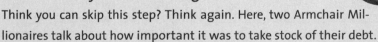

Debt Buster #1 in Practice—Tips for Dealing with the Day of Reckoning

Think you can skip this step? Think again. Here, two Armchair Millionaires talk about how important it was to take stock of their debt.

The Debt Hit List

"My husband is a spender—he never met a new gizmo or gadget he didn't feel he needed to have and saving was a totally foreign concept to him. I, on the other hand, am a saver and can pinch a penny until it begs for mercy. I handle all the finances, and I would feel guilty if I had to tell him, 'No, we can't afford it,' or 'Money is tight.' But I was about to tear my hair out, because I would pay off a bill only to find out he'd charged it back up again.

"To finally get him to participate and pay attention, I made up a 'Debt Hit List.' I listed all the debts, balances, monthly payments, and interest rates. I wrote down everything, even mortgage and utilities. I also included income compared to expenses. Then I showed him the list. He was in absolute and total shock and finally understood why there was no cash flow. He finally turned over all his credit cards, and with his newfound cooperation we were finally able to make progress. Last year we paid off eleven debts in twelve months and this year we have paid off six. We now have cash flow and he is much better about his spending habits. It just took the shock of it all in black and white to wake him up. I wish I had thought of the hit list idea five years ago."

—Armchair Millionaire member debsan

Psych Yourself Up

"I started reducing my debt by writing down everything I owe. When I did it, I was appalled at my situation. It helped me realize that I will never learn to be responsible for my finances if I don't act. I got myself in this mess. I will feel so proud and accomplished once I get myself out of it."

—Armchair Millionaire member MsJoeCool

Now, gather up all your credit card statements for the past few months, your car loan, student loan, and mortgage payment books, and any other related paperwork. Make a list of all your debts, including the balance of each debt, the minimum payment due right now, and the interest rate.

If you're unsure of any of these items, call the toll-free number that you'll find on your statement to get all the information.

Have you ever seen your own credit report? For a serious reality check, you might want to get a copy of the information that's been reported by credit card companies to various credit reporting companies. If you've been having trouble making payments on time, or have built up a mountain of debt, it could be sobering to see it all on paper in black and white. Some Armchair Millionaires get really motivated after they've seen the hard evidence of overspending.

It typically costs about $8 to get a copy of your report from one of the major agencies, and you can get one free if you've been denied credit for any reason. For more information, or to order a copy of your report, contact one of these agencies:

Experian
P.O. Box 2104
Allen, TX 75013-2104
888-EXPERIAN
http://www.experian.com

Equifax
P.O. Box 740241
Atlanta, GA 30374-0241
800-685-1111
http://www.equifax.com

Trans Union
P. O. Box 403
Springfield, PA 19064
800-888-4213
http://www.transunion.com

Another good resource for information on obtaining and understanding credit reports is available on the Quicken.com Web site:
http://www.quicken.com/banking_and_credit/credit_reports

Why is this step so important? You won't win this battle unless you know exactly what you're up against. Besides giving you a baseline reading of your personal debt situation, this information will be essential for planning your investing strategy.

One more note: This is a time of reckoning, so try to be completely and totally honest with yourself.

Defeat Your Debt Worksheet

Go ahead—write in this book! This isn't second grade, so there's no teacher to reprimand you. If you'd like, go ahead and make a copy of this page (you might need more than one), or recreate it with a spreadsheet program in your computer. Then, gather up those monthly statements, and fill out this form. You'll use this list later during Step 6 to help plan your strategy.

DEBT NAME: Credit Cards, Loans, etc.	CURRENT BALANCE	MINIMUM PAYMENT: Monthly	INTEREST %	COMPANY INFO
Visa	$5,000	$125.00	13.9%	MBNA VISA 123 Debtfree Way Wilmington, DE 67890 800-800-0000 Acct. # 123-1234-12-1234
Car Loan	$2,250	$300.00	7.7%	ABC FINANCE 456 PayLater St. New York, NY 12345 888-800-0000 Acct. # 123-1234-12-1234

Once you've completed your list, you may find it completely overwhelming. But please don't despair. Standing face to face with the enemy may be intimidating, but it's necessary.

Now let's figure out how to knock this mountain of debt down to size.

DEBT BUSTER #2: INVEST IN YOUR DEBT. If you sit down and add it all up, you'll probably be surprised to realize how much you're paying in interest every year, just from carrying balances on your credit cards from month to month. Starting right now, however, you're going to think about your monthly payments in a different light. Instead of being an albatross around your neck, think of those monthly payments as an investment in your future. We call this "investing in your debt."

Even though it might hurt when you write out that check to the credit card company, you need to speed up repayment of your debts. Figure out how much money you can invest in your debt each month, over and above the regular monthly payments you are making now. It could be a single lump sum payment, or an extra monthly payment on your auto loan or mortgage. Chances are that you'll probably need to make a commitment to paying a higher amount for several months, or even for a year or two. Commit as much as you absolutely can. Even if you can only find an extra $10 a month you will be able to make a difference.

Debt Buster #2 in Action—Making a Molehill out of a Mountain

Here are some ideas from Armchair Millionaires to help make those aggressive payments just a little easier.

The Methodical Method

"After you've come up with your list of debts, pick one card (I usually pick the one with the smallest balance) and concentrate on paying it off. When it is paid off, close it out, and work on the next one. The fewer bills you have coming in, the less stressful it is and the easier it is to keep track of what you owe so you can plan."

—Armchair Millionaire member Kitkatson

Make Your Payments Online

"I have signed up for online bill payment. I've got a lot of debt. I hate paying bills, so I was often late with the payments. Last year I paid almost $600 in late charges alone. Now with the online payments, I just set up recurring payments and all I have to do is log on once in a while and all my credit cards (as well as some of the other bills) are paid."

—Armchair Millionaire member vizsla

Really Assess Your Priorities

"Very often we think about getting out of debt as requiring huge sacrifices—cutting back on things that you enjoy or feel you need. When things feel like a sacrifice, we naturally don't really want to do them. I have found that once I start to think about getting out of debt not as a sacrifice but as a priority, something I truly want to do, the whole picture changes. Suddenly when I choose to not buy something, it doesn't feel like I'm denying myself anything, but instead like I'm investing in myself, and in the dream of being debt-free. I think this attitude shift has really made me feel like I'm much more in control of my debt and my financial future, rather than feeling like a victim."

—Armchair Millionaire member bandl

Why is it important to invest in your debt? If you make only the minimum payments on your cards, your progress on paying them down will be very, very slow and expensive. If you have a $3,000 balance on your credit card and only make the minimum payment of $10 each month (or 2 percent of the total, whichever is higher), it will take you almost thirty-eight years to pay it off! And it will cost you $7,931 just in interest.

DEBT BUSTER #3: LESSEN THE BURDEN. You may have been surprised to see the interest rates charged by your credit cards when you filled out the chart. Credit card companies are great marketers, but you'll never hear one tell you how much one of their "exclusive preapproved titanium" cards will really cost you if you carry a balance from month to month.

But you'd better pay attention to the rates on cards you carry. Just think about that $7,931 you could potentially owe on a $3000 balance with an 18 percent interest rate. If you switch to a card with a 9.9 percent interest rate, you'll pay down the debt three years sooner, and pay just $1,935 in interest—a savings of nearly $6,000.

It just doesn't make sense to carry a balance on a card with a high rate if you can transfer the balance to a card that charges a more reasonable interest rate. You may also be able to consolidate your credit card debts by combining the balances of two or three cards onto a single card with a lower rate.

You may be able to get your credit card company to knock down your interest rate a point or two. How do you get them to do this? Simple—just ask. A phone call to your credit card provider with a request for a lower rate is often all it takes to pay less in interest each month. If you want to find a card with a lower rate, that's pretty easy, too—try using the Web. You can search on the Web for a credit card with the right rate for you:

BankRate.com
11811 U.S. Highway 1
North Palm Beach, FL 33408
561-627-7330
http://www.bankrate.com

BanxQuote
305 Madison Avenue, Suite 5240
New York, NY 10165
212-499-9100
http://www.banx.com

ABC Guides Credit Card Rates Guide
http://www.abcguides.com/creditcards

Also, magazines such as *Money* regularly publish lists of the best
credit card rates.

Usually, you apply for a new card with a phone call, or even online.
Just remember that card companies sometimes offer a lower "teaser
rate" at the beginning, but the rate may balloon to as much as 21 percent after the teaser period ends. As always, check the details before
you sign up.

Debt Buster #3 in Action—Minimizing the Credit Card Bite

Credit card companies can be sneaky, but that's no reason not to
enlist their help. Below are ideas from the Armchair Millionaire community on using credit card companies to your advantage, as well as
some warnings about what to look out for.

It Works!

"I called four creditors today and two of them lowered my interest
just because I asked them to."

—Armchair Millionaire member LittleEd

Some Words of Caution

"Once credit card companies catch on that you're paying them down they'll increase your credit line and decrease your minimum payments. Don't fall for it. Once you put your plan together, stick with the original payments. One card chopped my minimum in half! They also happen to be one of my highest interest balances. I just keep jabbing away at it using the same payment amount I started with."

—Armchair Millionaire member gbchriste

Terminate Unnecessary Cards

"You don't have to wait until your card is paid off to close the account. By closing the account, or 'suspending account privileges' as they might say, you still make your payments each month but you won't be able to charge and you won't see a renewal card show up in the mail one day. One less temptation to face! A nice side effect of attempting to close your credit card account might be more favorable terms. When they ask why you are closing, tell them the interest rate is too high. If they transfer you to a special accounts representative, you've got them on the hook. Most likely, they will offer either a permanent or temporary rate reduction. Great! Take the lower rate and cut up your card anyway."

—Armchair Millionaire member cstephenso829

And remember: Signing up for more credit cards doesn't mean that you get to spend more. In fact, you should cut up your old cards right away, and notify the credit card companies that you're canceling your account. Holding on to unused credit cards can limit the amount of credit you can get in the future, and it might make it too easy to succumb to temptation if some big-ticket item catches your eye. One warning is in order: Don't try to do the credit card shuffle. Some people are constantly switching from card to card in search of low rates. When the teaser rate expires, they switch to a new card. If you do this too frequently, the card companies will catch on, and you might find a dark spot on your credit report.

Refinance Your Mortgage

Another strategy for reducing your debt is to refinance your home mortgage. Armchair Millionaire member Marla M. and her husband had an adjustable rate mortgage (commonly known as an ARM) on their South Carolina home. As the name implies, the interest rate on an ARM is adjustable—but you don't get to change the rate, only your bank can. And, as Marla discovered, your bank is likely to raise it at any chance they get.

When Marla purchased her house, her rate was an affordable 6.25 percent. Three years later, her rate had increased to 7.87 percent, significantly increasing her monthly mortgage payments. So she went mortgage shopping. Using the Web, she found a fixed-rate thirty-year mortgage that would lock her in to a 6.87 percent rate.

While that 1 percent difference doesn't sound like much, it came out to $83.33 a month for Marla, a savings that can really add up over the years. Over the thirty-year duration of the loan, the savings will amount to $8,143.

But the really amazing thing about that $83.33 is that it could have a big impact on that monthly house payment. If Marla applied that amount directly to the principle on her home, she could pay off the loan in twenty-two years instead of thirty! An even more exciting prospect is the idea of investing the monthly savings in a long-term saving and investing plan. If Marla invested according to the strategies laid out by the Armchair Millionaire, and can achieve a 10 percent annual return on her portfolio, that $83.33 per month would grow to $173,267 at the end of the thirty years!

Sure, it's a hassle to refinance your mortgage. But when interest rates are low, it can also be a very smart thing to do. You can reduce your overall debt load and free up some cash to pay down other debts, or to save and invest for your future.

Don't Be Driven by Car Loans

The funny thing about buying a new car is that as soon as you drive it off the dealer's lot it becomes a used car. And its value drops by as much as 30 to 40 percent! Meanwhile, you're still facing four years of monthly payments.

Unfortunately, you won't be able to refinance your auto loan like you can with your home mortgage loan. You might be able to make additional payments on the loan, paying it down as quickly as possible.

The real opportunity to save comes when you make the purchase in the first place. There are a few rules that Armchair Millionaires use before making one of the biggest purchases of their lives—an automobile.

- Always buy used. Since a new car becomes used as soon as you buy it, why not just buy a used car at the start? You'll save lots—and you won't have to go so deeply in debt (if at all).
- Go for practicality, not style. That sport utility vehicle may make you feel great, but a sensible sedan will get you to your destination at the same time without burning a hole in your wallet.
- Buy with cash, not with credit (as much as possible). Whenever you are able to save in order to make a big purchase you'll come out far ahead of borrowing.

DEBT BUSTER #4: GIVE UP PLASTIC FOR ONE WEEK—AND FOR GOOD. So the real clincher of this debt-reducing strategy is that once your debt is gone, *you can't go out and rack up new debt.* This is not a one-time deal. Your attitudes about spending have to change. This all sounds very scary, but to get started, all you have to do is give up plastic for one week. Still sound scary? Many Armchair Millionaire members thought so too—they all decided to give up their credit cards for the same week during the "Declare War on Your Debt" Community Challenge. And you know what? Nobody died from a lack of recently charged consumer goods. In fact, a lot of people got really excited about the possibility of life without debt—permanently.

You can try this too. Make a promise to yourself to give up credit cards for one week. Take the cards out of your wallet, and lock them up. Some people put all their credit cards into a bowl of water and then put the bowl in the freezer. Now, if you want to buy something with your card, you really have to think about it while the ice is thawing!

Without easy access to your credit cards, how do your spending habits change? For most people, the realization that you *can* live without credit cards is somewhat shocking, but also a step in the right direction.

Debt Buster #4 in Action—Make Your Experiment a Success

Okay, so you're not carrying around your credit cards. Congratulations! However, there are still other pitfalls to avoid. Here, Armchair Millionaires explain how they've made the most of going without credit.

Beware the Debit Card

"I finally had a lightbulb go on over my head. We stopped using our credit cards some time ago and have been using checks and a debit card for everything. It finally occurred to me that we were having trouble paying the bills, not because we don't make enough money, but because we haven't been careful about where we were spending it. We weren't charging things, but the debit card was a little too convenient. We started figuring out how much money we need to put aside each payday for the bills (including saving) and take out the rest in cash. So after we pay bills, there's not a whole lot of money left each week. That money is used for groceries, entertainment, and miscellaneous expenses. Once the money is gone, it's gone and we have to make do until the next payday. It doesn't leave much room for error, but we have our savings account for backup."

—Armchair Millionaire member lucifie

Eliminate Temptation

"If you can't control yourself at the store, don't go. The more you shop, the more you think you need. Find another source of entertainment. Take pride in going without things; it makes you feel good. You can handle this."

—Armchair Millionaire member judycater

Whatever It Takes

"When I was paying down my credit cards, I would remind myself that credit cards are not our friends. Think of them as little plastic gremlins sitting in your wallet. While you sleep at night those little plastic gremlins come to life with razor-sharp teeth and a huge appetite and gobble up all the cash in your wallet and checkbook. When I kept that image in my mind, it made me think twice about reaching into my wallet to pull out a credit card and charge something. I know it's silly, but it worked for me—I couldn't wait to get those hungry little gremlins out of my wallet."

—Armchair Millionaire member debsan

Once you've learned that you can live without your credit cards for a week, try it for two weeks. Then try it for a whole month. Before too long, you'll break the credit spending habit altogether.

It can take time to really change your spending habits, but there are some tricks you can use to help rein in your urges. One way is to mentally add the amount of interest you're likely to pay on top of each purchase you make. That stack of new CDs might cost you $79.99 at the music store checkout. However, if you carry a balance on your 18 percent-rate credit card and make only the minimum monthly payment, the real cost of those CDs might be closer to $110. It would take you thirty-two months of making the minimum 3 percent payment to pay off that purchase, and you'd pay about $30 in interest. Are those CDs worth $110?

DEBT BUSTER #5: PLAN YOUR STRATEGY Now you're ready to really move into action. There are two plans of attack to paying down your credit card debts, and it's your choice which to use.

Using the list you made on page 44, find the card with the highest interest rate, and the one with the highest outstanding balance (after you've made any transfers or balances). Some Armchair Millionaires prefer to get rid of as many of their debt-laden cards as quickly as possible, so they choose the card with the smallest outstanding balance and direct their monthly "debt investment" (from Debt Buster #2) toward that card each month until it's entirely paid off. Then they cut up that card, notify the credit card company that they want their account cancelled, and proceed to the next smallest outstanding balance. You would proceed in this fashion until you've entirely eliminated all your credit card debts.

Armchair Millionaire Member Poll
How much credit card debt do you have?
45% Less than $1,000
22% $1000–$5000
15% $5000–10,000
18% More than $10,000

The average balance on a credit card in America is $7,000. Armchair Millionaires are beating those odds—with 45 percent carrying $1,000 or less in credit card debt. Where do you stand? If you're not one of those 45 percent, don't panic. Reading this book is your first big step toward getting there.

Others prefer to pay off the card with the highest interest rate first. Once you've paid down that card, move to the card with the next highest interest rate, and continue until you've eliminated all your debts.

If you've completed Steps 1 through 5, then you're ready to make a long-term commitment to reducing your spending, reducing your debts, and increasing your savings. But you also should not delay starting your own Armchair Millionaire Five Steps to Financial Freedom plan while you work down your debts. Even if you can put aside only $10 a week for your long-term savings plan, that's enough to get started.

Debt Buster #5 in Action—Other Benefits of Setting Goals

While all these steps to becoming debt-free may sound overwhelming, the word from Armchair Millionaires is that taking these steps can help change your whole attitude about the process of eliminating debt. And once you can see your debts in a different light, doing what you must to get rid of them isn't so hard after all. Here some Armchair Millionaires share their insights:

Attitude Adjustment

"My wife and I have discovered that assessing our situation has helped change our attitude toward spending. In fact, it is completely changed now that we have a set of clearly defined goals. We actually have these written down and I chart our progress on a set of graphs every month. Our top priority is to be debt-free in three years. We now use the phrase 'in three years' as a point of humor in our house. Whenever anybody says, 'I need such and such . . . ,' my wife or I will pipe up with, 'in three years.' It's amazing. Our sofa has a tear in it. My wife looked at it and said, 'I guess that can wait three years.' The VCR broke. 'We'll get another in three years.' The list goes on. Now that we realize what the benefits will be, three years just doesn't seem that far off."

—Armchair Millionaire member gbchriste

The Most Important Step

"I seriously thought about bankruptcy at one point—I was behind on my car loan, my rent, my credit cards. But I found that once I made my mind up that I was not going to let it all defeat me, I began to succeed in reducing my debt."

—Armchair Millionaire member brianpearcy

Where to Go If You Still Need Help

If you have tried the Armchair Millionaire plan for defeating your debt and still feel like you need more help, don't worry. There are a number of wonderful national nonprofit organizations devoted to assisting those with debt problems. The National Foundation for Consumer Credit and Myvesta are two excellent groups that will work with you and your creditors to allow you to pull yourself up out of debt. If you do sign up for one of their services, though, don't be surprised if the advice they give you sounds a lot like our advice in this chapter!

National Foundation for Consumer Credit
8611 Second Avenue, Suite 100
Silver Spring, MD 20910
800-388-2227
http://www.nfcc.org

Myvesta.org
P.O. Box 8587
Gaithersburg, MD 20898
800-680-3328
http://www.myvesta.org

The Final Piece—Finding the Support You Need

Perhaps the best part of the Armchair Millionaire Web site community is the inspiration you'll receive from the other people there who are also dedicated to getting their finances in order. Best of all, they are there at any time of the day or night so you can boost your resolve whenever you need to.

You Don't Have to Do It Alone

"My husband and I are working on overcoming our debt. At first we were very excited at the prospect of being debt-free. But then I started thinking it would take forever and I got depressed. But what has really helped to keep me on track is coming back to the Armchair Millionaire message boards on a regular basis. Every time I come here it helps me to realize my goals again, and I usually get off-line and write out another check to a credit card company."

—Armchair Millionaire member Junebugs

Chapter 4 Action Items

In this chapter, you have learned how to defeat your debt, a necessary step before starting to build your long-term savings plan. Here are the steps you need to get started.

- Make a list of all your debts, including credit cards, the amount owed on each, the interest rates you pay, and other details about the loans and cards. Set aside a monthly dollar amount to be directed at your debts.
- Reduce your debt burden by transferring balances to a credit card with a lower interest rate, or refinancing your mortgage, or consolidating your debts into a lower interest rate loan.
- Set aside a week when you won't make any charges on your credit card whatsoever. Don't carry them with you (not even "in case of emergency").

- Make a monthly payment to your creditors, starting either with the debt with the highest interest rate, or the debt with the largest outstanding balance. Then continue until you're debt-free!
- Finally, start your saving and investing plan right now, even if you're deep in debt. Learning to save can be hard, but it gets easier once you see your portfolio start to grow. To find out how to get started, go on to Part II: Five Steps to Financial Freedom.

Part II

....

Five Steps
to Financial Freedom

In the first part of this book, you heard from the real experts—the people who make up the Armchair Millionaire community—who attest that building a successful portfolio doesn't take a lot of luck or require a great deal of money. And you've learned that beginning your portfolio will require patience and discipline; it will be one of the most grown-up decisions you'll ever make.

Now that your head and your heart are ready for the road ahead, all that remains is finding out *how* to invest.

The five steps to building an extraordinary portfolio, even on an ordinary income, are the subject of Part II. As with Part I, you'll learn the tips, tricks, and wisdom from real Armchair Millionaires, but you'll also learn about a specific plan—the Five Steps to Financial Freedom. These five simple steps have been culled from the experiences of thousands of investors. They are the five most successful, powerful, and reliable saving and investing strategies ever. And they have been battle-tested by teachers, doctors, financial advisors, men and women, novices and experts alike. In short, these five steps can make you a millionaire.

The Five Steps break down like this:

- The first two steps, *Max Out Your Tax-Deferred Savings* and *Pay Yourself First,* are simple savings techniques that will show you how to hold on to enough of your income using tax-advantaged investing and simple budgeting tricks to begin investing.
- Step three, *Invest Automatically,* and step four, *Use the Armchair Investing Strategy,* show you how to invest your savings in the stock market using the strategies that have made investors wealthy for decades. Pay special attention to Chapter 4 where we reveal specific portfolios and investments that can be tuned to your personal investing goals and time frame. With these model portfolios, you can put your plan into action today with confidence and knowledge.
- Finally, in step five, *Start Today,* we reveal the most important secret to building wealth. Without a doubt, this is the one strategy that all successful investors have in common. And best of all, it's easy to implement.

You're only five steps away from financial freedom. Take a deep breath, and get ready to take your first step now. . . .

CHAPTER 5

STEP 1:
Max Out All
Tax-Deferred Savings

There is a revolution going on. One that you, yourself, may be part of. And you might not even know it.

It's a retirement savings revolution. Millions of Americans are behaving like savvy investors by using special savings plans to build a substantial nest egg that will fund their retirement years. These investors are saving vast wealth (to the tune of an estimated $4.5 trillion) using retirement plans sponsored by their employers or the government (or both). They are taking advantage of government programs that are designed to help them save money and reduce their taxes at the same time.

We all know that Americans tend to gripe about the government. And we all want to reduce our taxes. Armchair Millionaires know that the first, most important step toward building a nest egg is to max out all the tax-advantaged retirement plans available to them. If you decide to take the government up on one of these plans, you're getting in on a terrific deal. Not only will you be saving for your own future, the government will give you a break on your taxes, or at least let you postpone paying some of them for twenty or thirty or forty years. Just think how much your money could grow in that time!

There are a number of different retirement plans that you might be eligible for depending on whether your company offers a plan to its employees, whether you're self-employed, what your annual income is, and other factors.

What Makes a Retirement Account a Retirement Account?

The first thing you need to know is that many of these government-approved plans all use something called "tax-deferred" investing.

Hold it right there. What does tax-deferred mean, you ask? "Tax-deferred" is actually an accountant's term, and it means that you can get out of paying some taxes now, though you will have to pay them later. With tax-deferred accounts, you get to kick in money on a regular basis, let it grow, and postpone ("defer") any taxes you might have to pay until your retirement years.

All these plans share at least one of the following characteristics:

- Ability to make pretax contributions, meaning whatever money you put into a retirement account is put in before taxes are taken out. Therefore, retirement account contributions lower your tax bill right away.
- "Tax-deferral," the postponement of all taxes on earnings in the plan until retirement. At retirement, when your income will probably be lower, you'll pay taxes at a lower rate.
- Elimination of all taxes on earnings in the plan. You may never pay taxes on the earnings in some retirement plans!

Of course, the downside of these specialized retirement plans is that you have to be willing to put the money away until you're almost sixty years old.

If that seems like a long time, don't worry, because you get plenty of benefits from retirement accounts in the short term, too. For example, by taking money out of your paycheck and socking it into a 401(k) or traditional IRA, your monthly tax bite will go down. That's because the IRS looks at tax-deferred money as if it weren't really earned, and therefore, no taxes are owed. Overall, the benefits of tax-deferred savings are mighty substantial.

How much will all this save you? Lots. Here's an example using a 401(k), a company-sponsored retirement plan that might be one of your options:

Let's say you contribute $2,000 to your regular (as in not tax-deferred) saving and investment plan at the beginning of each year. If your account can grow just 10 percent a year, you'll end up with $596,254 in thirty-five years. But you'll have to pay taxes along the way on all the dividends, interest, and capital gains that you earn in this account. Those taxes could take a formidable bite out of your portfolio's performance. If taxes eat up just 1 percent of your return each year, your nest egg in thirty-five years turns out to be just $470,249 (say goodbye to $126,005—yowza!).

So what happens if you put $2,000 into a tax-advantaged retirement account instead? First of all, you can kick that expected return back up to 10 percent, ending up with $596,254, since you won't have to worry about paying taxes each year in the account. But it gets even better when you add in the savings you'll get on your federal income taxes. If you're in the 28 percent tax bracket, a $2,000 contribution to your retirement plan could save you $560 a year in taxes. For the same out-of-pocket cost to you of $2,000 a year, you could be putting aside $2,560 into a retirement plan. So once you factor in the growth of that $560 you save each year, the end result of all this accelerated saving is a grand total of $763,205 in thirty-five years.

ADVICE FROM RICH

"Think of retirement account investments as a gift from Uncle Sam. If you contribute $2,000 to a tax-deferred account, you not only get $2,000 working for you, but you save $560 on your tax return. So it's as if you received $560 for free. And how can you turn down free money?"

When you retire, it's true that you'll have to pay taxes on the money as you withdraw it from your account, but the assumption here is that you'll be living on an income that's smaller than when you were working, and therefore you'll be in a lower tax bracket.

From the Armchair Millionaire's Gallery—
Meet Crystal R., Who Learned to Love Her Retirement Plan the Hard Way

Instead of lecturing you about how important retirement savings are, we're going to let one of our community members show you how learning to save for retirement is an important part of growing up.

Armchair Millionaire Member Name: Crystal R.

Age: 27

Hometown: Brooklyn, NY

Occupation: Proposal writer for management consulting firm

Family Status: Married

Financial Goals: Comfortable retirement, financing kids' college educations

How Did You Get Started Investing?

Very simply, my company offered a 401(k) program. I was so impressed by the company's matching agreement of 14 percent. And I thought, "Wow, this can't be real!" So I did the max. I was twenty-four at the time. I chose the fund that was most aggressive. I felt that I had little or nothing to lose and I felt like I was of the age where I could invest a sizable amount and if things didn't work out in the first couple of years, eventually things would balance out and I'd be okay.

What happened when you noticed your paycheck was less when you began your 401(k) program?

Once I did it, I forgot about it. I'd get my statements and check the balance and get excited, but that's pretty much it. What impressed me the most was that I could invest a certain amount of money but it wouldn't result in an equal amount decrease from my paycheck because it was a pretax investment. So I could invest just over $200 and only feel the difference of maybe $180 plus the company matching. It was incredible.

What's the Biggest Investment Mistake You've Made?

I made a huge one. When I changed jobs, I never rolled over the money I had put away into my 401(k). Instead, I spent it all. I don't even remember what I spent it on. Don't get me wrong, I enjoyed spending it. But I should have been more serious about what that money was intended for. I won't be doing something like that again.

What Did You Learn from That Mistake?

I wish I had more discipline back then. I have it now. A lot of the realities of life have sunk in over the last few months. Saving money has become much more important to me. My father had a stroke recently. Watching him go through both physical changes and financial strain from not being able to work have made me realize that you've got to be prepared for anything. That event made me much more serious about saving and investing.

What Do You Want Others to Know About Starting to Invest?
There's a huge difference between just saving and saving to invest. My philosophy used to be, "Let me save so I can spend." But that's not what investing is all about. Unless you can connect it to a larger event—like retirement—you sort of miss the point. People know this, but there's a difference between knowing and doing.

A Short History of Retirement Plans in America

Before we get into the specific plans and how each one could work for you, here's a short history of how these plans came about in the first place.

One of the first people to suggest an all-encompassing retirement plan in America was Revolutionary War figure Thomas Paine, way back in 1795. (It's just a coincidence that Paine's best known work is titled "Common Sense," the phrase that Armchair Millionaires use to describe their investing strategy.) Paine proposed a 10 percent inheritance tax to fund a program that would pay annual benefits of ten pounds sterling to each citizen after turning fifty.

Paine's plan was never enacted, of course. But in 1935, another government-sponsored plan was created to provide for the security of older Americans, aptly named "Social Security." The goal of the system was to "give some measure of protection to the average citizen and to his family against the loss of a job and against poverty-ridden old age," as President Roosevelt said when he signed the legislation that passed the Social Security Act into law.

Social Security was never intended to allow retirees to live "high on the hog," however. It was meant to keep those who were no longer able to work off the soup lines, and as a result only provides a very modest income. (Those of you who are expecting Social Security to carry you through your retirement years may be in for a rude shock.)

The Future of Social Security?
ADVICE FROM RICH

In a recent survey of Americans aged eighteen to thirty-four, 46 percent believed in the existence of extraterrestrials while only 28 percent believed Social Security will still be around when they retire. But what are the facts? Andrew Hacker, author of *Money: Who Has How Much and Why*, explains it this way: "Figuring out whether Social Security will be able to support you when you retire is a simple thing. How many workers are there per retiree? Because Social Security is taken from your check, it spends three months in Maryland, and then it goes out to your grandfather. When Social Security started, there were something like twelve workers to every retiree. We're getting dangerously close to two to one. And that's the wake-up call for individual investors to plan on being responsible for their own incomes when they retire."

In decades past, employees could count on their companies to provide for a comfortable retirement. After a lifetime of service, a "company man" was sure to receive a gold watch and a pension that would see him and his wife through their golden years.

Corporate pension plans are known as "defined benefit plans" because they pay out a fixed amount to retirees, based on a formula that considers the person's salary history, age, and number of years of service. The company puts up the money that funds the pension plan for all its employees, and then invests that money until it's needed.

But back in the 1980s, some big companies were having trouble with their pension plans. Specifically, they weren't putting enough money in the plans to cover the payouts they'd need to make to their current employees upon retirement.

Of course, companies that engaged in the practice of underfunding their retirement plans were faced with the wrath of their employees—and, in many cases, the powerful unions who represented those workers. What could be worse than reaching retirement age and learning that there's nothing left in your company's pension fund for you?

As a result, a new type of company-sponsored retirement plan began to emerge in the 1980s. A corporate benefits consultant named Theodore Benna pored over the U.S. tax code trying to figure out ways that employers could provide cash bonuses or profit-sharing plans to highly paid executives without discriminating against low-level staffers. Benna discovered a loophole in paragraph (k) of section 401 that could be used to turn profit-sharing plans into tax-deferred savings plans, and the "401(k) plan" was born.

401(k) plans are retirement plans offered by companies to their employees. In these plans, the workers must make contributions to the plan from each paycheck (from their pretax salary, thereby lowering their tax bill). The company may or may not make an additional matching payment, too.

Companies like 401(k) plans, and one reason is because they shift the cost of retirement plans to the employees. As a result, fewer companies are offering pension plans these days, and more companies are offering 401(k) plans.

If your company doesn't offer a 401(k) plan, don't worry. In 1974, the U.S. tax law was modified to allow individuals who weren't covered by a company pension plan to save for retirement and still get a tax break. These plans are known as Individual Retirement Accounts (or IRAs).

Millions of Americans have established IRA accounts, which offer the opportunity to set aside money before taxes, like a 401(k) does. The money you invest in the IRA account gets to grow free from taxes until you retire, just like a 401(k). You can open an IRA at just about any bank, brokerage firm, or mutual fund company. When you retire, you can begin to take money out of your IRA, paying taxes as you go.

Congress introduced a variation on the IRA in 1998—the Roth IRA. The Roth IRA, like a "traditional" IRA, lets your money grow free from taxes until you retire. But unlike a traditional IRA, the money you withdraw from a Roth IRA is completely tax-free! Of course, the U.S. government isn't going to give up on collecting taxes altogether, so you won't get a tax break up front when you contribute to a Roth IRA (like you get when you fund a regular IRA).

Armchair Millionaire Member Poll
Which Retirement Account Is the Fairest of All?

We aren't the only ones who think that 401(k)s are great. When we asked the Armchair Millionaire community where they had their retirement funds, here's what they had to say:

Where will most of your retirement income come from?
43% 401(k)
25% IRA
23% Pension
8% Social Security

MAKING THE MOVE TO MAXIMUM SAVINGS

With all these retirement plan options available, how do you figure out which is best for you?

When it comes to retirement and tax-related investing, there's a lot of information to consider. So we've brought it all together into one special section.

This will make it easier to learn about the topic—when you're ready. If you're not prepared to dig into this information just yet, feel free to jump ahead to Chapter 6. There, you'll be able to continue learning the simple steps you need to take in order to achieve financial independence the Armchair Millionaire way.

When you've finished the book, you can return to this section to learn how to maximize every last dollar of your tax-advantaged savings and investing and put your plan into action!

Uncover the Right Retirement Plan for You

Do you have a job? Then your first stop on the retirement plan highway should be to march into your company's human resources department to find out if they offer a retirement plan for employees—and if you're eligible! Chances are good that your company has a 401(k) plan available to its employees.

Signing up is as simple as filling out an enrollment form that tells your company how much you want to have withheld from each paycheck and deposited into your 401(k) account. That's it! (Well, you'll also have to figure out how to invest your funds, but we'll cover that in Chapter 8.)

The Beauty of the 401(k) Plan

401(k) plans are an Armchair Millionaire's best first choice for long-term savings, for a couple of reasons:

1. Once you establish your account, your company will handle all the details of putting money into the plan—automatically! You won't have to remember to write a check or transfer money each month.
2. 401(k) plans provide tax savings from federal income taxes by letting you fund the account from pretax earnings. In other words, the money you contribute to your 401(k) will be taken out of your paycheck before any other deductions or taxes, so you'll see the

tax savings in each paycheck. If you decide to set aside $50 from each week's paycheck for your 401(k), and you're in the 28 percent tax bracket, your check will only be $36 smaller—not $50!

3. You won't have to pay any taxes on the earnings and gains in your 401(k) until retirement. This will allow your portfolio to increase in value over time at a much faster rate.

A Real Life Look at the 401(k)

Think the money that you stash away in a 401(k) won't amount to much? Here, Armchair Millionaires explain how the money can add up, and how to make the most of your 401(k) funds.

401k All the Way

"A 401(k) plan is an excellent way to save for retirement. Nothing yet (except winning the lottery) can beat it. I know! I've been in my 401(k) since 1983 and I can't believe how it's grown—way up there in the six figures! All I can tell you is, do it!"

—Armchair Millionaire member arnawaz

Maxing Out from the Get Go

"When I became eligible for my 401(k), I took the plunge and went for 15 percent right away instead of trying to work up to it. I had to work a moonlighting job for a while, but now I am accustomed to less money in my hand. I have learned to love paying myself first!"

—Armchair Millionaire member caugros

4. Many companies will match the contributions that employees make to their 401(k) plans. Your employer might kick in fifty cents for every dollar you contribute up to a certain point, or they might even match you on a one-to-one basis. Armchair Millionaires have a name for this—it's called "free money"! When you think about it, you'll find few opportunities in your life when people

will pay you for taking care of yourself, so you should never pass up an offer like this from your employer. In fact, a cardinal rule of 401(k) saving is to always contribute at least enough to your plan to get the maximum match (if your company offers one).

Many companies have specific "sign-up" periods for 401(k) plans, such as once a quarter. That's one reason it's important to get started in your 401(k) as soon as possible. If you miss the sign-up period, it might be another three months before you'll be able to get started.

Many companies have a waiting period of six months or a year before employees are eligible to participate in their 401(k) plans. If you're waiting to become eligible, there's no reason you can't start saving now, though. Figure out how much you'll contribute to the 401(k) and then set that money aside in a separate savings and investment account when you receive each paycheck.

How Much Can You Contribute to Your 401(k)?

You can contribute up to 15 percent of your pretax earnings, to a maximum of $10,500 a year (in 2000—the amount is adjusted for inflation each year). Some company plans will even allow you to make extra, nondeductible contributions to your 401(k) above and beyond that 15 percent limit. Generally, though, you'd want to make sure that you have taken advantage of any other tax-advantaged retirement plans that you are eligible for before making nondeductible contributions to a 401(k).

One final thought for those of you who might be wary of locking up your money for the next forty years: Many 401(k) plans will allow you to borrow money back from your account, and then repay yourself with interest. You might be able to borrow up to 50 percent of the value of your account, and repay the loan with your regular contributions. Just remember that borrowing from your 401(k) means that you'll have less money working toward meeting your ultimate retirement goals, so consider this as a last resort if you really need the cash. It might provide some peace of mind, though, if you anticipate the need to come up with a down payment for a home or cover big tuition bills for your kids.

But just don't plan to take the money out of your 401(k) before age fifty-five. If you do, you'll be subject to a 10 percent federal penalty tax, probably a state penalty tax, and payment of the income taxes that you deferred when you put the money into the plan in the first place. This can take a hefty bite out of your total proceeds.

Learning the Hard Way

The thing about retirement plans is that you really need to wait until you are legally retiring to dip into that money. Is it really so bad if you don't wait? See what this Armchair Millionaire has to say:

The Best Laid Plans . . .

"Word to the wise: Don't withdraw from your retirement plan! Everyone advised me against it, but I'm hardheaded and had to do it my way. Now, I'm slapped with a huge tax bill. I had my reasons for making the withdrawal at the time, and had my plan worked out, I would've been able to pay this tax bill. But, as we know, the best-laid plans don't always work out. Anyway, just take my advice and DON'T DO IT!"

—Armchair Millionaire member donyale99

Company-Sponsored Alternatives to the 401(k)

If your company doesn't offer a 401(k), they might offer a 403(b) or 457 account instead.

A 403(b) account is very similar to a 401(k), except it's offered to employees of schools, universities, and nonprofit organizations. 403(b) accounts are somewhat more limited than 401(k)s in the types of investments they can hold—403(b)s have to be invested in mutual funds or annuities (a type of insurance plan). They are sometimes known as tax-sheltered annuities (TSA).

A 457 plan is a deferred compensation plan offered to government employees, and offers the same pretax advantages as a 401(k). The maximum amount is 33⅓ percent of your predeferral taxable compensation or $8,000 (in 2000). It's possible that you might have a 401(k) and 457 plan available to you and can contribute to both.

If you work for yourself, or for a small company, your employer might offer you a retirement account such as a SEP-IRA, SIMPLE IRA, or Keogh plan. The principle behind all these plans is exactly the same—you and/or your company can contribute pretax money to your retirement account, getting a tax break and allowing your money to grow unimpeded by taxes.

A Keogh plan (also known as a Qualified Retirement Plan, or QRP) is designed for a self-employed individual or small business. There are two kinds of Keogh plans, "Profit Sharing" and "Money Purchase." If you establish a Money Purchase Keogh for your business, contribution is mandatory—you must make the same percentage contribution each year (up to 20 percent of your income, up to a maximum of $30,000)—whether you have profits or not. In a Profit Sharing Keogh, contributions are limited to the lesser of $30,000 or 13.04 percent of your self-employment income. The contribution percentage can change each year. Individuals can contribute to both types of plans in the same year.

A Savings Incentive Match Plan for Employees (SIMPLE), allows companies with 100 or fewer employees to offer a SIMPLE IRA plan. With this plan, employees can defer a portion of their salary as with a 401(k), up to $6,000 annually, and may receive an employer match or contribution as well.

In a Simplified Employee Pension (SEP) IRA, employees can make generous tax-deductible retirement contributions (up to $24,000 per year) for themselves and any employees. This is the easiest and most economical business retirement account to set up in most cases.

In fact, if you have a moonlighting job, or have any self-employment income at all, you ought to consider establishing a SEP-IRA or other retirement plan specifically designed for small businesspeople. A SEP-IRA is easy to set up with just about any brokerage firm or mutual fund company. Even if you have a 401(k) at your day job, you can contribute to a SEP-IRA. And since SEP-IRA plans let you stash away much more each year than in a 401(k) plan, that $24,500 limit is something to strive for.

Other Retirement Plan Options—
The Individual Retirement Account

Once you've contributed the maximum to any company-sponsored retirement plans such as the ones we've just described, it's time to take a look at some other options that might allow you to shelter your money from taxes. If your company doesn't offer any retirement plan for its employees, then you'll definitely want to take a look at Individual Retirement Accounts (IRAs).

An IRA is a special account that you establish with a bank, mutual fund company, or brokerage in which you can save funds for retirement.

The tax-cutting benefit of an IRA makes it particularly appealing to many investors. If your adjusted gross income (AGI, the amount of your annual income that the IRS uses to determine the taxes you owe) is below a certain level, and you aren't covered by a pension plan or a retirement plan at work, then you can deduct your IRA contributions from the amount of your income that's subject to federal income taxes, lowering your tax bill.

The amount that you are allowed to put into your IRA is also determined by your AGI. If your AGI in 2000 is less than $30,000 for a single taxpayer or $50,000 for a married couple filing jointly, you can deposit up to $2,000 (each, if married) as a deductible contribution. The amount that can be contributed and deducted is scaled down for single people who make up to $40,000 and for couples who earn up to $60,000.

Making Contributions the Easy Way

One reason a personal IRA isn't quite as alluring an investment vehicle as a 401(k) is that no one is going to make automatic contributions for you. So you could get to the end of the year and have to make a lump contribution of $2,000, and not everyone has $2,000 sitting around. Here, two Armchair Millionaires tell us how they got around that:

Funding an IRA the Easy Way

"I have found that using direct deposit from my employer helps me to save for retirement. I have $166 taken automatically from my account monthly and put into an IRA (multiply that times 12 and it adds up to $2,000). Some employers will let you split the direct deposit (money market and checking, for example). Just ask; even if they don't tell you, they may offer it."

—Armchair Millionaire member mtnspirit

You Don't Need Cash to Open an IRA

"Some of the fund companies, such as Fidelity or Scudder, for example, let you open IRAs with stocks instead of just putting cash in. I have bought stocks and used the dividend reinvestment provision. The results have been excellent."

—Armchair Millionaire member rfd21

If you're not eligible to make a deductible contribution to an IRA, it is possible to make a contribution to a "nondeductible IRA." Nondeductible contributions still grow tax-deferred in the IRA, but withdrawals after the age of 59½ are taxable only on the gains in the portfolio—you already paid the taxes on the original contributions. In a fully deductible IRA, contributions and earnings are entirely taxable because 100 percent of the original contributions provided a tax deduction to the individual.

When Can You Withdraw Funds from an IRA?

The main advantage of an IRA is that you pay no taxes on gains in the account until you retire. This is why IRAs are referred to as "tax-deferred" accounts. Taxes on dividends, interest, and capital gains are all deferred, in the case of an IRA, until retirement. When you eventually do retire, you can begin to withdraw money from the account and use it to augment your income from Social Security and other retirement plans. At that time, you'll pay taxes on the funds you take out at the IRS's "regular income" tax rate.

One warning about IRA withdrawals: Generally, if you take out funds from your IRA before the age of 59½, you'll pay a penalty. However, you can withdraw funds from a regular IRA without penalty for the following reasons:

- You buy a first home (up to $10,000)
- You need to pay for qualifying higher education expenses (for you, your spouse, your children, or your grandchildren, to pay for tuition, fees, books, supplies, and equipment)
- You need to pay medical expenses that are greater than 7.5 percent of your AGI
- You need to pay health insurance premiums because you are unemployed
- You become permanently disabled
- You roll over the distribution to another IRA
- You are withdrawing funds using a special schedule of early payments made over your life expectancy (IRS rules allow you to begin withdrawing funds prior to age 59½ in the form of an annuity that is paid at least once a year. The amount of that annuity is set by IRS rules based on your life expectancy and cannot be changed once payments have begun.)

There are many complicated rules about IRA accounts, but the bottom line is that by letting your funds grow tax-free over a long period, you can build a substantial nest egg for your retirement.

Remember, IRAs are designed to help you plan for a comfortable retirement—they lose their benefits if you tap into the account too soon.

A New IRA Option—The Roth IRA

In 1998, Congress introduced the Roth IRA. This is an IRA with a twist—the funds you deposit into a Roth IRA grow on a tax-free basis in the account until you withdraw them, but when you do take out the money, you won't have to pay any taxes on the earnings you've accumulated. In a regular IRA, funds grow on a tax-deferred basis, but when you withdraw money from a regular IRA, you have to pay taxes on the withdrawal as regular income.

How is this feat accomplished? The initial contributions you make to a Roth IRA are made with after-tax dollars—they are nondeductible. You don't get a break on your tax bill when you put money into a Roth IRA as you do when you contribute to a regular IRA. The break comes later, when you don't have to pay any taxes on the money you take out.

ARE YOU ELIGIBLE? If your 2000 AGI (adjusted gross income) is more than $160,000 (for a married couple, filing jointly) or $110,000 (for a single individual), you can stop reading right now; you're not eligible to make any contributions to a Roth IRA this year.

If your AGI is $150,000 or less (married, filing jointly) or $95,000 or less (filing singly), then you can contribute $2,000 per spouse to a Roth IRA. You can contribute to a Roth IRA even if you or your spouse is covered by a pension plan or by a company retirement plan like a 401(k).

If your AGI is between $150,001 and $160,000 (married, filing jointly) or between $95,001 and $110,000 (filing singly), the amount you can contribute is gradually phased out.

While Roth IRAs allow you to withdraw money before retirement under certain circumstances, there are special rules that govern when you can take money out and what you can use it for. If you don't follow the rules, you could be liable for a penalty tax.

Every IRA is made up of two types of funds: *contributions,* the money you put into the account, and *earnings,* the amount of any investment gains that your contributions have made while in the account (sometimes known as accumulated earnings). Earnings that you withdraw from the IRA are known as *distributions.*

You can take out *contributions* at any time from a Roth IRA without penalty and without any tax liability. Not that you'd want to take out those contributions—after all, it's the power of compounding that can really build up your portfolio over a long period of time. But, it's nice to know that you have access to some cash in case of a big emergency.

After a five year period, you can withdraw the *earnings* that have accumulated in your account without taxes or penalty, but only for the following very specific "life changes":

- You reach the age of 59½
- You (or your spouse, children, or grandchildren) buy a first home (up to $10,000 only)
- You become disabled
- You die

One difference between a Roth IRA and a traditional IRA is that upon your death, your heirs would receive your Roth IRA proceeds entirely free from federal income taxes, whereas, in a regular IRA, your heirs would be liable for taxes on the total amount of your account.

Any earnings taken out of your IRA for the above reasons and after the five-year period are known as a *qualified distribution.*

If you withdraw earnings for any reason other than those listed above, you'll have to pay federal taxes at your regular income tax rate and a 10 percent premature withdrawal penalty. This is called an *unqualified distribution.*

PENALTY-FREE DISTRIBUTIONS. You can avoid the premature withdrawal penalty in some instances. Roth IRAs have provisions that give you a break on the penalty in the case of some other "life changes." You are exempted from the penalty, but not from the taxes, if you take out earnings from the account for the following reasons:

- You need to pay medical expenses that are greater than 7.5 percent of your AGI
- You need to pay health insurance premiums because you are unemployed
- You need to pay for higher education expenses
- You buy a first home (for amounts over the $10,000 tax-free allowance)

POTENTIAL PITFALLS. Another point is worth mentioning here: Any withdrawals you make are treated as coming first from your contributions. You can't choose whether to withdraw earnings or contributions—you must take out the money you put in first, and then take out the earnings. While this isn't a problem in most cases (since your contributions can be accessed without penalties and taxes), it may make a difference when planning withdrawals in some circumstances.

One more thing. States don't always follow changes in federal law, so there may be state taxes on accumulated earnings that are withdrawn from a Roth IRA, whether or not they are free from federal taxes. You'll need to check with the department of taxation in your state to see how they handle these distributions.

The bottom line is that Roth IRAs offer a totally tax-free way to save for retirement. In addition, in many instances you can have access to the money in your account prior to retirement with no penalty and little or no tax liability. With the Roth IRA, Uncle Sam has given Americans a nice break and an important new retirement planning tool—with the flexibility to help you handle important life events along the way if you need to.

How to Choose

So how do you choose the retirement vehicle for you? Remember, there are really three options when choosing an individual retirement account: a deductible IRA, a nondeductible IRA, and a Roth IRA. Your total annual contributions to any single type of IRA or a combination of a Roth IRA and deductible IRA can be no more than $2,000, subject to AGI (Adjusted Gross Income) limits. And you must have earned income to contribute to any IRA (meaning that you must have gotten your income from a job, and not an investment portfolio).

SHOULD YOU CHOOSE A DEDUCTIBLE IRA OR NONDEDUCTIBLE IRA? If you are eligible for a deductible IRA, it's always a better choice than a nondeductible IRA because the contributions provide a tax deduction in the current year. Nondeductible IRAs are okay for people who have already contributed the maximum to all other retirement plan options and still want to put money away for the long term.

SHOULD YOU CHOOSE A ROTH IRA OR NONDEDUCTIBLE IRA? A Roth IRA will always be a better choice than a nondeductible IRA (an IRA that is funded with after-tax dollars). Contributions in both accounts grow on a nontaxed basis, but the earnings distributed from a nondeductible IRA when you retire are taxable at your regular income tax rate. Remember, your distributions from a Roth IRA are tax-free.

SHOULD YOU CHOOSE A ROTH IRA OR DEDUCTIBLE IRA? Roth IRAs have fewer limitations on participation than deductible IRAs. It's possible that you might have an AGI that's too high to allow you to contribute to a deductible IRA, or that you're covered by your employer's pension plan or 401(k). In either case, a Roth IRA will be an obvious choice.

However, the choice between a Roth IRA and a deductible IRA is less clear for many people. Some experts claim that you should always take a tax deduction when it's available to you—which means choosing a deductible IRA, rather than a Roth IRA.

The issue of "getting your tax benefit up front" is what most differentiates a Roth IRA from a regular IRA. The Roth IRA is described by the Internal Revenue Service as a "back-loaded IRA" because its tax benefits are only fully realized when money is withdrawn from the account. A regular IRA is "front-loaded" because you realize a tax deduction in the year in which you contribute to the fund.

The problem with figuring out which IRA is best for you is that you need to determine whether the "back-loaded" tax benefits of a Roth IRA (which you'll realize twenty or thirty or forty years down the road) outweigh the "front-loaded" benefits of a regular, deductible IRA. Here are a few things that you should consider when making your choice.

> If you're feeling confused about whether a Roth is for you, join the club. When we asked the Armchair Millionaire community if they converted to a Roth, there was no one clear winner.
>
> *Did you convert to a Roth IRA?*
> Yes 45%
> No 55%

Ben Franklin's famous words, "Nothing is certain but death and taxes," are certainly true. But there's no way to be absolutely sure of the tax rates to which you'll be subject when you retire. One thing you can be sure of is that our elected representatives will continue to fiddle with the tax code, raising and lowering the tax rates over the years.

Leaving the uncertainty of changes in the tax code aside, the major consideration in choosing between the two types of IRAs is what tax bracket you expect to be in when you retire, and if that is higher or lower than your current bracket.

How Others Have Made the Decision

You may be scratching your head right now, wondering how you'll be able to figure out which IRA is best for you. Here, two Armchair Millionaires share their insights on how to decide.

Run the Numbers

"Anyone who is considering a Roth needs to contact a financial advisor and have them run the numbers. How much will your future wealth increase by switching to a Roth? More importantly, how much will it cost to switch, and can you afford the current tax liability? My wife and I both have traditional IRAs worth about $35,000 each. My financial advisor ran the numbers and found that by the time we reach fifty-nine and a half our savings would be twice that of a traditional IRA if we switched to a Roth, but that it would cost about $15,000 in current taxes to switch. That's money we don't have, and to take it from the IRAs as they currently stand would defeat the purpose of the IRA. The good news is you don't have to switch all of your money to a Roth, you can convert as much or as little as you like. Regardless, the best retirement planning advice is to get started right away."

—Armchair Millionaire Loco

You Could Keep Your Old IRA and Put Future Funds into a Roth— Avoiding the Taxes Due in a Roth Conversion

"It's tough for a lot of people to come up with the taxes due in a Roth conversion. But if you are saving money for retirement every year anyway, putting new money into a Roth IRA has some tremendous advantages over the long haul, since the earnings are all tax-free. Even if you can afford to only put a few bucks a year into a Roth IRA, just do it. You won't regret it ten or twenty years from now."

—Armchair Millionaire member Larry

IF YOU EXPECT YOUR TAX BRACKET TO BE LOWER IN RETIREMENT.
One of the assumptions that has made a deductible IRA such an attractive retirement planning vehicle in the past is that your federal income tax rate will be lower when you retire than when you are working. Say you are currently in the 28 percent federal income tax bracket. When you retire, it's likely that you will be living on a reduced, fixed income, and that your tax bracket will drop to the 15 percent level. The distributions you take from that IRA are taxed at 15 percent instead of the 28 percent you might have paid prior to retirement, a significant savings.

For that reason, if you and your spouse expect to be in a lower tax bracket during retirement, the traditional IRA will generally be a better deal than a Roth IRA. You'll get big tax deductions now while you are in a high bracket, but pay much lower taxes on your IRA distributions later when you are in a low bracket.

The presumption in this recommendation is somewhat unrealistic, however. First of all, taxpayers in a "high tax bracket" (at the top of the 28 percent bracket and above) are unable to contribute to a deductible IRA, and so aren't getting "big deductions."

Secondly, comparing a Roth IRA and a deductible IRA is a bit like comparing apples and oranges, since one provides you with a tax benefit today, and the other provides you with a tax benefit when you retire. In order to make a fair comparison between the two types of IRAs, some mathematical adjustments are necessary.

One complication comes when you compare a Roth IRA and a regular deductible IRA. When you calculate how much you'll be able to contribute before taxes to a deductible IRA, you should plan to invest the money you "save" on taxes in a separate, non-tax-advantaged brokerage account or mutual fund. That's because you'll eventually have to pay taxes on your contributions to your IRA. With a Roth IRA, it's too easy to forget that you've already paid taxes on the money you've deposited into your account, but those taxes are a real expense. By investing the "tax savings" from a deductible IRA, you may find that you will come out ahead with a deductible IRA. Unfortunately, investing those tax savings is something that most people won't do.

If you expect your tax bracket to be lower in retirement, and you don't invest the tax savings provided by the deductible IRA contributions each year in another account, and you still want to maximize your after-tax retirement income, a Roth IRA will likely be a better choice.

IF YOU EXPECT YOUR TAX BRACKET TO BE HIGHER IN RETIRE-MENT. If your retirement planning has been moving along nicely, it's probably not hard to imagine a scenario in which your income when you retire may actually be higher than it is now, moving you into a higher tax bracket. If you expect to be in a higher tax bracket at retirement, then a Roth IRA is probably the better choice. You'll get to lock in the tax rate you pay right now. Later, when you're sitting pretty in a higher bracket, you won't have to worry about the tax man at all!

What's Your Tax Bracket?
ADVICE FROM RICH

You'll hear lots of talk about "tax brackets" whenever retirement plans are discussed. But do you know what your tax bracket is, or how to figure out what it is? It's simply the federal income tax rate you'll pay to the IRS each year, based on your AGI (that's your Adjusted Gross Income, your taxable income base). The following table outlines the federal income tax brackets from 2000; someone who is in the "28 percent tax bracket" has an AGI of between $25,351 and $61,400 (if they're single) or $42,351 and $102,300 (if they're married and filing jointly).

2000 Taxable Income Brackets and Rates

Single	Married Filing Jointly	Federal Tax Rate
$0–$26,250	$0–$43,850	15%
$26,251–$63,550	$43,851–$105,950	28%
$63,551–$132,600	$105,951–$161,450	31%
$132,601–$288,350	$161,451–$288,350	36%
Over $288,350	Over $288,350	39.6%

IF YOU EXPECT YOUR TAX BRACKET TO BE THE SAME IN RETIREMENT. The choice becomes less clear, however, if you expect to be in the same federal tax bracket at retirement. In most cases, identical amounts invested in a Roth IRA and a regular IRA that achieve the same rates of growth will end up roughly the same value after taxes. In such cases, you'll probably prefer the Roth IRA, since you'll get tax-free instead of simply tax-deferred earnings. In addition, Roth IRA holders have an increased accessibility to funds in the account under certain circumstances. That advantage may tip the scales further in favor of the Roth IRA.

Wrapping Up IRAs

Many brokerage firms and mutual fund companies provide IRA calculators on their Web sites, and sometimes offer workbooks and other materials that can help determine what plan is best for you. Often they'll send you a complete retirement savings kit along with the application forms you'll need. Check the Appendices at the back of this book for phone numbers and Web site addresses to get in touch with these firms.

One terrific online source of information about IRAs is the Roth IRA Web site (http://www.rothira.com). This site has articles, links, and calculators to help you figure out all the details of retirement plans.

While all this talk about Roth IRAs and traditional IRAs may be confusing, just remember this: It's far more important that you are putting money aside into some kind of retirement plan than which plan you're using. Banks, brokerages, and mutual fund companies are among the most common places to have an IRA. You can also invest your IRA in CDs, bonds, stocks, mutual funds, limited partnerships, and certain types of real estate. (We'll give you the lowdown on the best investing approach for Armchair Millionaires in Chapter 8.)

You have until April 15th to open or deposit money into an IRA for the prior tax year. Even so, you should try to make your annual IRA contributions as soon as possible at the beginning of the year, not at the end of next March. Better still, you can set up an automatic transfer to have money sent electronically from your bank account to your IRA account each month or each quarter. This ensures that you'll never have to remember to write a check or worry about coming up with a big chunk of money for your annual IRA contribution.

Chapter 5 Action Items

In this chapter, you've learned why you should max out all your tax-deferred savings plans. Here are the steps you need to take to get full advantage of all the options available to you.

- Talk to your boss or human resources department about the company retirement plans they may offer employees.
- Sign up for your 401(k) or other company plan, and make it your goal to contribute the maximum amount that's allowed.
- Set up an IRA or Roth IRA account, if you're eligible. You can open an account at just about any bank, brokerage firm, or mutual fund company.
- Establish an automatic investing plan to have money sent to your IRA account each month.

CHAPTER 6

STEP 2:
Pay Yourself First

A Method to Save Big Money Without Budgeting All the Fun Out of Your Life

If you make an annual salary of $35,000 a year, and work for thirty years, you'll have earned more than one million dollars (even if you never get a raise). But the big question is, how much of that million will you be able to save?

There's a simple method that will help you to hold on to some of that cash painlessly. By the end of this chapter, you will have learned the secret to becoming a world-class saver. And don't worry, you won't have to take a vow of poverty in order to begin building your savings. But you will have to adapt how you approach saving for the future. You see, the problem with thinking that you don't have enough to start your savings plan is that you've put the most important person in your life—yourself—at the bottom of your list of priorities.

But What About the Bills?

This is a common complaint that we hear from people who haven't started their own savings plan yet. "Sure, I'd like to build up my savings account," they say. "But after I put food on the table, pay my mortgage, make the car payment, and take care of all the monthly bills, there's barely anything left for the fun stuff. If I started saving money, I'd have to live like a monk."

ADVICE FROM RICH

Every schoolkid knows that Ben Franklin wrote "A penny saved is a penny earned." While that simple bit of advice is usually used to admonish people to start stashing pennies in the piggy bank, that's missing the point. The real gist of this maxim is that if you spend every cent you bring home, you aren't really earning anything because you end up giving all your money to someone else. Only when you pay yourself can you really consider that money "earned."

Sure, all those things like rent or the mortgage, groceries, the electric bill, medical bills, the car payment, the gas bill, the water bill, property taxes, and so on are important. Nobody's saying you should skip the phone bill in order to put a few extra dollars in the bank; in fact, telephone companies tend to look askance at customers who don't pay their bills, to put it mildly.

And yes, you should be able to buy yourself a new sweater, or CD, or whatever, from time to time. But the thing about saving money is that it's not about deprivation. If you put aside money that you would normally spend on something else (say those frothy, tasty, and expensive cappuccinos you indulge in every day on your way to work), then you're substituting cappuccinos now for a big, juicy bank account later. A bank account that you can use to buy something big—like a house. Or a second house. Now doesn't that make up for all those missed cappuccinos?

Repeat After Us: Budgeting Stinks

The second problem most people face when trying to start saving comes from listening to the standard advice they get from investment books and financial advisors. According to these "experts," before you do *anything* else with your financial plan, you should sit down and come up with a monthly budget. List all of your expenses on one half of a piece of paper (this is the long list) and all your income on the other half (this is the short list). Add up all your monthly expenses, and subtract them from your monthly income, and the result is the amount of money you should be able to save each month. If you end up with a negative number, then reduce your expenses in appropriate places until you end up with more income than expenses.

Now (or so the theory goes), you have a plan to follow for all of your monthly spending. Many experts recommend that you carry around a little notebook and write down every dime that you spend each month. At the end of the month, add up all you've spent and you'll know exactly where all your money went.

While this exercise is supposed to provide you with a road map for building up your savings, all too often it proves to be *only* an exercise, and a futile one at that. Human nature always seems to get in the way. Despite all their good intentions, too many people fall flat on their faces. Within a few weeks, they've abandoned their budgets altogether. Now, besides being right where they were when they started, they've concluded that they are destined for financial failure and will never be successful at this saving thing. Nothing could be further from the truth—at least if you take a few tips from the Armchair Millionaires.

Real Life Ways to Get a Grip on Spending

You can sit in your chair reading this book and say to yourself, "That's it! From now on, I'm saving money!" This would be fine if you were going to spend the rest of your life sitting in that chair. But sometime soon, probably today, you're going to find yourself in some sort of store. It may be a grocery store, it may be the mall, it might even be Neiman Marcus. And then the resolve you've just built up may waver—even the tiniest bit—and the next thing you know, you've dropped a wad of bills on a new, improved razor, or fabulous pair of shoes. . . . Here, fellow Armchair Millionaires share their strategies for taming the spending monster.

How Many Hours Will It Cost?

"One thing that does work for me is to calculate how many hours it will take to earn the after-tax and post-pay-yourself-first money to buy the item I'm pining for. When I realize that an item will take a month to earn, I often reconsider."

—Armchair Millionaire member kimberly

The Waiting Game

"What works well for me is to write down the price of every item I am tempted to buy. I then slip the list back into my purse. I review it every week. Occasionally, I realize that something on the list will truly enhance my quality of life, so I go ahead and buy it. (Two examples of this are my computer and my treadmill, both of which I use daily.) However, most of the items on the list I find that I really don't want once the initial impulse is gone. I have actually saved thousands by using this method."

—Armchair Millionaire member Mew

An Enveloping Financial Plan

"We are paid twice a month so I write two checks each month for cash. The cash goes into envelopes for school lunches, allowances for the children and my husband and me, and for entertainment (such as movies and dinners out). When the set amount of money is gone, it is gone. But I always feel satisfied because we have enjoyed ourselves without wrecking our financial plan."

—Armchair Millionaire member anonymous

Numbers Don't Lie

"My biggest temptation is clothes. I have a closet crammed full of them, but always feel I have nothing to wear. Here's how I reined myself in: I reviewed my credit card bills for the past five years, and added up the cost of every single piece of clothing I'd ever bought (I always bought on credit). I could not believe how many thousands of dollars I'd spent on clothes, yet I hardly liked anything I owned! I calculated what that money would be worth if I'd put it into a mutual fund and got really depressed. But it helps me put my spending into perspective and makes clothing sales a lot less tempting."

—Armchair Millionaire member anonymous

You can understand why Armchair Millionaires have a motto that they proclaim often and loudly: "Budgeting stinks!"

Believe it or not, you don't need a budget to be able to build up your savings. You don't have to write down every dime you spend in a little notebook (even though some people find this a good deterrent to overspending). In fact, you probably already have a very good idea of your own spending habits.

How to Pay Yourself First

To get yourself headed in the right direction, you need to do one thing: Move yourself up the priority list. In fact, you should move yourself all the way to the top of the list, right to the number one position. Each month, before you pay all the essential and nonessential bills in that stack on your desk, write a check to yourself earmarked for your future. Make it out in the amount of 10 percent of your monthly take-home pay (take-home pay is the amount of your paycheck after taxes and all other deductions). And put this in the memo field on the check: "For my financial freedom plan."

Then, send that check to a separate account—preferably a saving account that you can't access through an ATM machine—before you have a chance to spend it. We call this "paying yourself first," and it's the Armchair Millionaire's alternative to not paying yourself last. In time, your savings will grow and help you become a wealthy person.

Getting back to that 10 percent, you may wonder why you should set aside 10 percent of your paycheck, as opposed to 8.5 percent or 15 percent? Well, it's a nice round number and it's easy to calculate, to be sure. But when you really think about it, would giving up 10 percent of your salary really cramp your lifestyle? Check out the chart to see what you would have to give up in a typical month in order to reach eventual financial success. Most people find—much to their surprise—that they can get by quite comfortably on a salary that's 10 percent lower.

What would you have to give up to "Pay Yourself First?"

If you make $45,000 a year, and pay roughly 30 percent of your salary in taxes and other payroll deductions, your take-home pay would be about $2,625 a month. Ten percent of your monthly take-home pay comes out to $262.50.

So what does that mean in the real world? Here's what you'll have to give up in a month in order to pay yourself first and begin your path to financial independence:

$2.25	3 Cups of coffee or tea
$6.00	3 Muffins to go with that joe or tea
$3.00	3 Chocolate chip cookies from local bakery
$3.00	6 Hershey chocolate bars
$9.00	2 Big Mac Value Meals at McDonald's
$8.00	1 Latest Mary Higgins Clark or Tom Clancy paperback
$25.00	1 Latest Danielle Steel or John Grisham novel (hardcover)
$3.50	1 Latest issue of *Maxim* or *Elle* magazine
$4.00	4 Bottles of Bud (watching the game, at home)
$6.00	2 Bottles of Bud (watching the game, at a bar)
$6.00	4 Espressos

$25.00	2 Latest Faith Hill or Moby CDs
$50.00	1 Newest shoot 'em up computer game on CD-ROM
$12.00	3 Pay-per-view movies on cable
$16.00	2 Movie tickets at the nearest multiplex
$17.50	5 Video or DVD rentals at Blockbuster
$15.00	1 Large Papa John's pizza with the works, delivered
$7.00	2 Gallons of ice cream (the cheap stuff)
$7.00	2 Frappuccinos at Starbuck's
$6.00	2 Bags of Oreo cookies
$6.00	1 Dozen Krispy Kreme doughnuts
$8.00	2 Bags of chips and french onion dip
$6.00	2 Fruit smothies
$11.00	11 Instant lottery tickets

$262.25   Total

How much beer, ice cream, and magazines would you have to give up each month in order to save 10 percent of your paycheck? You can see for yourself on the Armchair Millionaire Web site, at: http://www.armchairmillionaire.com/fivesteps/step_2app.html

Plug in your take-home pay, and the calculator will do the rest!

The not-so-highly-technical term for this strategy is, "Pay Yourself First." Once you understand the concept, it makes perfect sense, right?

At the very beginning, you might find it hard to adjust to living without the money you're saving and investing. Over time, though, most people discover that they don't really miss the money that's being whisked out of their account each month. It's hard to miss something when you haven't even seen it in the first place. And if you should happen to run out of money at the end of the month, you'll have already set aside the money for your saving plan.

Tips for Putting "Pay Yourself First" into Place

Paying yourself may make a lot of sense logically, but when the time comes to actually take that money out of your checking account, it can seem like a crazy idea. Below, Armchair Millionaires share their tricks for making sure that you don't miss that 10 percent.

I'm Just a Bill

"As soon as I get paid, I put money away for my bills. I also have to pay myself just as if I had gotten a bill in the mail. Add yourself to your monthly or weekly bills and soon it will be second nature to pay yourself."

—Armchair Millionaire guest

No Pain, All Gain

"When you get used to paying yourself first, the plan seems to run itself, unlike dieting or exercise. All you have to do is start. I hate exercise because of the true motto—no pain, no gain. With 'Pay Yourself First,' once you start, that's really all you have to do."

—Armchair Millionaire member Sean

There is one warning that comes along with paying yourself first. Just because you're not living within the constraints of a monthly budget that's been configured to the penny doesn't mean you have free rein to spend all you want. This is especially true when you're just getting started, before you've accumulated a lot of money in your account. Later on, when you've accumulated a few hundred— or a few thousand—dollars in your account, you'll see how your money grows and grows. That can be a real motivator when you're tempted to buy that king-size candy bar—just think about how every dollar contributes to your financial future.

As one Armchair Millionaire pointed out a few pages back, one way to change your spending habits is to stop thinking about the dollar amounts. Instead, think about how long you have to work before you'd make enough to pay for a particular item out of your "Pay Yourself First" plan.

Here's how it works. If you make $45,000 a year, your weekly paycheck of $865 is probably only worth $600 or so after taxes. Ten percent of your weekly take-home pay is $60, the amount you should aim to put into your pay-yourself-first plan.

Now, if you're thinking of buying a stereo that costs $300, how long would it take to pay for it? It would take five weeks' worth of paying yourself first in order to get your hands on that stereo. Dinner and a movie for two wipes out half a day's worth of savings. Opting for the $30,000 luxury car instead of a vehicle with a more reasonable price tag $18,000 might give you a flashier ride, but the extra $12,000 will cost you two hundred weeks' worth of paying yourself first.

Being Financially Responsible Doesn't Have to Be Boring

You don't need to budget all the fun out of your life, but you just might find out that you like the idea of spending less. There's a movement in this country of people who are dedicated to the idea of living well on less. For these folks, "frugal living" and "cheapskate" aren't derogatory terms, but labels that celebrate the notion of simplifying their lifestyles. These people have reevaluated their priorities, and decided that "simple" is better. They've figured out that they get around town in a 1995 Ford Taurus just as well as they would in a brand-spanking-new $49,000 luxury sedan. Or, they think it might be nicer to retire at age forty-five than to buy a big fancy house in a country club development (with a big mortgage to match) and toil away in their job until they're sixty-two just to pay off the home loan.

Having Fun with Less Money

Still think paying yourself first means you'll have to live like a monk? Try to look at it in a different light. This Armchair Millionaire member has found a way to do just that.

Reassess Your Priorities

"It helps to slow down and think about what you really want out of life. The answer for most people is not more stuff, but quality time and experiences with family, friends, and self. So skip the Saturday trip to the mall for clothes that you probably don't really need, and take the kids for a bike ride instead. Don't spend $20–$30 on a trip to the movies, go to the park and fly kites. Save the money and use it to get out of debt or to invest in your future and your children's futures. Choose to live more simply and you may just find that can save money *and* be happier."

—Armchair Millionaire member anonymous

The Difference Between Paying Yourself First and Saving for Retirement

It's also important to note that your "Pay Yourself First" plan is not a replacement for your retirement savings plan. You still need to be saving and investing in a tax-deferred retirement account, such as an IRA or 401(k). The money in your own savings plan can help you save for your other goals, whether it's the education of your child, a new home, an early retirement, or for any other dreams you may have.

"Paying Yourself First" is a layaway plan for your future—and you owe yourself a good future. And best of all, "Pay Yourself First" will grow your nest egg without changing your lifestyle.

From the Armchair Millionaire's Gallery— Three Folks Who Are on Their Way

Still need a little inspiration to start your savings plan? Meet three Armchair Millionaires who not only talk the talk, but walk the walk. They don't live like monks, they weren't born with trust funds, but they *are* working toward achieving all their financial dreams—just like you will when you start paying yourself first.

Looking to the Future

Armchair Millionaire Member Name: Glenda J.

From: California

Age: 45

Occupation: City government worker

Family Status: Divorced

Investment Goals: To invest for the long term and accumulate enough money to retire comfortably so I can travel, spend time with my kids and grandkids, and just have fun and not worry!

Background: I have never been a saver. I wish now that I'd started saving in my twenties—now that I'm in my mid-forties, retirement is making me nervous. I would like to retire by the time I'm sixty but I'm not sure that's feasible.

I had $10,000 in cash three years ago and it went to my head. My children and I just went on a spending spree. We had always had such a hard time—never having money, never being able to do fun things. So we bought new TVs, I fixed my ailing car, I bought another car (bad move—had to sell it later at a loss!), paid off bills, fixed my daughter's car, pretty much just frittered the money away. After eighteen months, it was gone like the wind. Now, in hindsight, I should have purchased stocks or mutual funds. I'll probably never have that much cash in my hands again.

I got started investing six years ago by putting money each payday into the tax-deferred program available through my work. Since then, I have seen my account go from $6,000 to $50,000. Several quarters I saw earnings of over $1,000 each. That was nice!

My daughter is now a single parent in her mid-twenties and I stress to her to save, save, save. She has opened a money market account at her bank. I tell her that if I had saved beginning at her age, I would probably have close to $500,000 instead of the $50,000 I have now.

I'd like to tell everyone who hasn't started their investment plan that you need to look to the future. Twenty years has a way of just going by and before you know it, you could be seriously thinking of retirement and worrying that you may wind up living on the street.

Some people are disciplined and save. I have never been that way. It has been a long time coming—but putting my money away on payday before I have a chance to spend it has really helped my portfolio grow.

Living Frugally But Still Having Fun

Armchair Millionaire Member Name: Mark P.

From: Oregon

Age: 28

Occupation: Mechanical Engineer

Family Status: Single

Investment Goals: Retire from the corporate world at 40

Background: Working in the high tech-industry, I make a good salary. But I live well below my means. I drive an inexpensive car and I don't eat out a lot. I get a kick out of being frugal, but I still dedicate funds to my favorite hobbies—windsurfing, snowboarding, and world travel. My goal is to remain debt-free until I make the inevitable decision to buy a house.

My dad was a real saver and taught us to do the same. My company offered a class called "The Road to Financial Independence" that I attended when I was twenty-four. That got me started investing. Before that, I thought that buying things would make me happy. I get a lot more enjoyment now out of watching my portfolio grow with companies I like than I do buying more stuff that I don't really need. I see that my friends have lots of debt that they can't seem to shed because they live consistently above their means. I've learned it's important to live simply and challenge yourself to be frugal . . . but not at the expense of having fun.

Setting Attainable Goals—and Reaching Them

Armchair Millionaire Member Name: Greg F.
From: Florida
Age: 44
Occupation: Salesman
Family Status: Married
Investment Goals: Retire at 52
Background: Pay yourself first. That's all you need to know. My father was a banker who grew up in the Depression. He taught me to live within my means, never carry a balance on credit, and encouraged me to go into business for myself, starting when I was eight years old selling pachysandra plants that I had grown, door to door. I still have a copy of the first paycheck I received.

I figured out how much I need to retire on and what my anticipated return is and then decided what I needed to save in order to accomplish that. I've tried to pass along what I've learned about saving and investing to my two kids, and recently gave them each a copy of *The Millionaire Next Door* to help them learn more about the subject. Probably the biggest event that has happened recently is my one-year-old marriage. I now have somebody I want to play and retire with. My wife, Gail, is helping to motivate me toward my goal.

Putting Your "Pay Yourself First" Plan into Place

Unfortunately, while the concept of paying yourself first sounds great, we all know how hard it is in reality to write that check to yourself each month. Let's face it. Budgeting, like dieting, just doesn't work.

If we all had that kind of willpower, America would be a country of healthy and wealthy folks.

Does that mean you should give up? No way. Here's how you can make sure you take care of your plan each month.

First of all, whatever you do, don't put your weekly or monthly 10 percent payment in a savings account that's linked to your checking account. That makes it too easy to transfer money back to your checking account, or to withdraw funds using an ATM card on the spur of the moment.

Ideally, you should open another, completely separate account, at a bank or other financial institution (we'll cover this in detail later in this chapter). If you think you might be tempted to withdraw money for some frivolous purchase, open an account at an altogether different bank from your regular bank, one that's on the other side of town or inconvenient for you to get to. You can mail your monthly check to the bank to have it deposited into your account. Don't get an ATM card, either. If your bank insists on sending you one, cut it into pieces right away or add it to that credit card sorbet in your freezer.

An Honest-to-Goodness Foolproof Plan to Pay Yourself First

There is one even easier way to pay yourself first each month—a method so foolproof that hardly anyone could mess it up. If you can't discipline yourself to pay yourself first each month, you don't have to stand alone. Call in the reinforcements!

Here's all you need to do: Get in touch with a brokerage firm or mutual fund company and open an account. That's not all, though. You need to ask the institution to help you pay yourself first, in what most financial institutions call an automatic deduction plan. (We like to call it the "Pay Yourself First Plan for Real People.")

Once you've set up your plan, your bank will send a specific sum each month to your mutual fund or brokerage firm. Automatically. Your broker or fund manager will then invest that amount on your behalf. Automatically.

Setting up an automatic investment plan is easy. Nearly all brokerage firms and mutual fund companies will help you. First, you need to have an account with a broker or mutual fund. If you already have an account, ask for an application form for their "automatic deduction plan." If you don't have an account, you can set up an automatic plan when you establish your account.

Complete the form and indicate how much you want transferred each month. Then return the form—you will generally be asked to enclose a voided check from your checking account.

Don't be confused about requests for the "routing number of your current financial institution" or other gobbledygook. A phone call to your bank or the financial institution can help fill in any blanks on the application.

One Automatic Plan Caveat

One of the great things about taking part in an investing community such as Armchair Millionaire is that you can benefit from others' mistakes. Here, an Armchair Millionaire community member explains one possible Pay Yourself First pitfall:

Don't Forget to Keep Track of Your Deduction
"You do, of course, have to remember to write the money that is automatically deducted in your checkbook each month so you don't bounce a check. Believe me, paying yourself is so easy. It is totally painless. Just sign up and you will naturally adjust your spending to accommodate the missing amount."

—Armchair Millionaire member Judy D

Chances are that you already have an automatic deduction plan in place to pay your monthly health club dues or life insurance premiums. Your 10 percent plan is no different.

It may take a month or so before your transfers start happening.

But after that, it's smooth sailing. Each month, your 10 percent will be electronically transferred from your bank account to your saving and investing account.

Let Your Employer Help

Many companies offer a savings plan for their employees, and this can be another good way to get started with your savings plan. Each week, your company will take a certain percentage from your paycheck and deposit it into a special account. Sometimes, you'll have the option of buying your company's stock in the savings plan. Other times, your money will simply collect interest or be available for investment into mutual funds. Check to see if your company offers such a savings plan.

Pay Yourself First Worksheet

After you've decided to pay yourself first, you need to figure out exactly how much you should be saving each month. Use this simple worksheet to determine your own monthly saving goal. A calculator might be useful if you're mathematically challenged, as many of us are.

ONE WEEK'S TAKE-HOME PAY $ _____

Take a look at your paycheck from last week. Try not to wince at the thought of all the taxes you paid. Now write the amount of the check, after taxes and deductions, on the above line. (If you get paid on some other basis rather than weekly, you'll have to make an adjustment.)

MULTIPLY BY 4.33 (x 4.33)

Seems like a strange number, doesn't it? Let us explain: Have you ever noticed how there are 52 weeks in the year, and 4 weeks in a month, but 12 months in a year? If you multiply 4 times 12, you end up with 48 weeks—not 52. That explains why you get your weekly paycheck 5 times in some months and 4 times in other months—the average month is actually 4.33 weeks long.

AVERAGE MONTHLY TAKE-HOME PAY = $ _____
If you multiply your weekly take-home pay times 4.33, the result is your average monthly take-home paycheck. Since we want to establish a monthly saving plan, this number is crucial.

MULTIPLY BY 10 PERCENT (X 10%)
Now, multiply your monthly take-home pay by 10 percent. *Monthly Amount to Pay Yourself First $ _____*
The result is the amount you should be setting aside each month in a separate saving and investing plan, on top of your contributions to an IRA and/or 401(k).

If 10 percent of your weekly paycheck seems comfortably within your reach, try increasing your monthly contribution to 15 percent. Also, when you get a pay raise, the first thing you should do is increase your weekly savings amount to 10 percent of your new paycheck.

There's no limit to how much you can save and invest, and the more you can put away on a regular basis, the better off you'll be when it comes time to reap the rewards.

Chapter 6 Action Items

In this chapter, you've learned the importance of "Paying Yourself First." Here are the steps you need to get started on your own "Pay Yourself First" plan.

- Set up a separate saving or investing account with a financial institution.
- Determine the dollar amount you will contribute each month. It's okay to start out small—but keep aiming to contribute at least 10 percent of your take-home pay in the plan.
- Establish an automatic deduction plan to transfer money each month from your bank to your saving and investing account.

STEP 3:
Invest Automatically—
and Benefit from
Dollar Cost Averaging

Now that you've learned some of the basic tools for saving money, it's time to get to the real meat of the matter—what to do with the money you've saved in order to achieve the maximum benefit for your long-term goals. While you might *feel* comfortable letting your money sit in the bank collecting interest, the danger in stashing your cash in savings accounts and certificates of deposit is that your money will only grow by 3 percent or maybe 5 percent a year. That's simply not enough to turn you into a millionaire.

Armchair Millionaires know that they need to do something with their cash besides putting it in the bank. But it's not good enough to simply "invest"—you need to invest in the most sensible fashion possible. So what are the options?

Coming to the decision to invest means knowing the answers to three simple questions.

1. **Where should you invest?** ("Stocks, bonds, or Treasury bills"?)
2. **When should you invest?** ("Is now the right time? Will the market go down soon?")
3. **What should you invest in?** ("If stocks, which ones?")

In this chapter, you'll learn the answers to the first two of these questions (we'll save the last question and the specific investment plan you should consider for the next chapter, Chapter 8). So let's take a look at deciding where you should invest.

Where should you invest?

As you might have guessed by now, Armchair Millionaires are partial to investing in the stock market. But stocks aren't the only place you can invest.

Experts divide the universe of potential investments into different categories called "asset classes." These groupings are just a way to lump together investments that have similar levels of risk and return. The three major asset classes are cash, bonds, and stocks. (Some people consider real estate, precious metals, and other natural resources as assets, too, but we'll stick with the first three classes.)

You're probably familiar with cash, even though you may never have thought of it as an asset class. Cash is just as good as, well, money in the bank—as long as you keep it in the bank and not under your mattress. The good thing about cash is that you can safely earn a little bit of a return in a bank account. The bad thing about cash is that you can only earn a little bit of a return in a bank account.

If your grandfather had put $1 in the bank on the first day of 1926, he'd have ended up with $16.06 by June 30, 2000. That's a 3.8 percent rate of return over 74 years. That's pretty dismal, but wait—it gets worse when you add in the effects of inflation. Inflation is nothing more than the rising costs of goods and services. Inflation is

a loaf of bread that costs $1.79 today, the same loaf that your mom used to buy for a dime or a quarter when you were a kid. Over time, inflation in the U.S. has grown at an average rate of 3.1 percent, and it impacts your investments just as it impacts the cost of bread. Adjusted for inflation, that dollar that your granddad invested in 1926 is now worth only about $1.67.

Armchair Millionaires know that it's a good idea to have some cash on hand for emergencies, but if you're working toward a goal that's twenty or thirty years down the road, it's better to seek out a better rate of return in another asset class. On the risk and return scale, cash offers little risk and little return compared to other investments.

So what about bonds? A bond is nothing more than a promise to repay a loan. The borrower can be a company (a corporate bond), a local government agency (a municipal bond), and even the federal government (a Treasury bond).

While many people think of bonds as "safe" investments, the riskiness of a particular bond depends on many factors, most importantly, who issued the bond. For instance, bonds issued by a company that's desperate for cash will pay a high interest rate, but that's because anyone who buys their bonds is taking the risk that the company will welch on the debt (this is known as "defaulting" on the bond). These are also called junk bonds. On the other hand, a bond issued by a company like IBM carries much less risk of default than a junk bond, so they can pay a lower interest rate. At the high end of the safety scale, bonds issued by the federal government carry little risk of default, since they are "backed by the full faith and credit of the United States government."

Are bonds a good idea? If your grandmother had persuaded her husband to buy long-term government bonds in 1926, their $1 would have grown to $44.24 by 2000, an average return of 5.2 percent. If she could have persuaded him to buy long-term corporate bonds instead, their $1 would have grown to $60.10, returning 5.7 percent annually. That's better than cash, for sure (way to go, Grandma!), but

after inflation it's hard to imagine that they could have really gotten ahead if they had stuck purely with bonds.

That leaves the third major asset class—stocks. Stocks are sometimes known as equities. These are shares of corporations that are bought and sold by investors in a public market. When you own shares of stock in a corporation, you become a part-owner of that company.

So let's say that Granddad invested in the stock market in 1926. Perhaps you're familiar with the history of the stock market and know about a not-so-minor event that happened in 1929 when the stock market crashed. What you may not know is that 1929 wasn't the worst of it. Over the next three years, the market continued to decline, making paupers out of millionaires. Granddad's $1 investment in 1926 would have been worth $2.20 at the end of 1928 (doubling his money in two years), but that $2.20 would have been worth just 79 cents at the end of 1932. Ouch!

But your granddad was smart. He didn't get spooked by the market, and he remained invested in stocks, even though there were many more times when the market would jump and fall dramatically. By mid-2000, his $1 investment would have been worth $2,833.51. We'll do the math here—that's an 11.2 percent annual return on his investment over the seventy-four-year period.

When you compare these three asset classes, the question about where to invest is a no-brainer. The stock market offers much higher returns over the long term, so most Armchair Millionaires invest their long-term savings in stocks. When we say "long-term" we mean five years or longer.

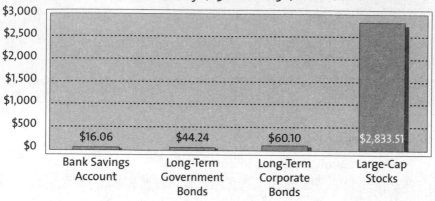

Growth of $1.00 Invested in Various Assets
January 1, 1926–June 30, 2000

But simply knowing that stocks are the place to be if you want to be a millionaire doesn't really go far enough. You still need to know when to invest in the stock market, and what stocks you should buy!

When should you invest?

Once you've made the decision to invest in the stock market, you need to know when is the best time to invest. When you look at the market from a historical perspective, you can see that it's very common for the market to experience some serious downturns. From 1928 through 1999, the Standard & Poor's 500, a leading index used to gauge the performance of the stock market (we'll tell you more about indexes in Chapter 8), declined in 20 of those 74 years. In 8 of those years, it declined more than 10 percent, and more than 20 percent in 4 of the years—and that's not even counting the times that the market has declined more than 10 percent or even 20 percent in the middle of a year and then recovered.

The stock market goes up and down in the short term without any apparent pattern or regularity, and it can be pretty painful to watch 30 percent of your portfolio disappear in the course of a couple of months. So what happens when the market falls through the floor?

Nothing.

The key to investing in the stock market is to remember that over time it always tends to go up. In 54 of the last 74 years, the S&P 500 has ended the year higher than it started out. In 43 years, the S&P 500 ended more than 10 percent higher, and in 29 years, it closed the year with a 20 percent or greater gain. As long as you're willing to wait it out, your portfolio should survive.

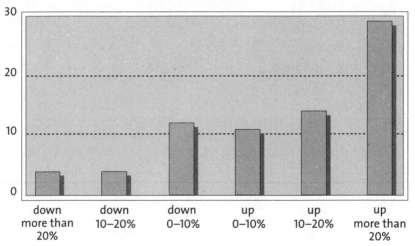

Number of Years in Which the S&P 500 Ended Year Higher or Lower than Beginning of Year 1928–1999

"So when is the best time to invest in the stock market?" you may be wondering. "When the market is high? Or when the market is low? And why can't I just sell right before the market drops and then buy back right before the stocks go back up again?"

Obviously, you'd love to be able to time your investments so that you only put money into the market when it's low. That way, when the market reaches new heights you'd make a fortune, right?

If only it were that easy. Unfortunately, there is no way of knowing when is the absolute best time to invest. Believe us, thousands of

people have searched and searched for the magic formula that would predict the direction of the stock market over the next day, week, month, or longer. All have failed. This is called "timing the market," and it's a waste of time. The truth is that no one is able to correctly guess the future direction of the market. Not your broker. Not the professionals of Wall Street. Not your Uncle Sid. No one.

Think about it: if there were a foolproof way of knowing exactly when you should buy into the stock market and when you should get out, we'd be a nation of millionaires already.

Another problem with trying to buy stocks in a falling stock market is that it sounds easy, but many people don't have the stomach for it. In fact, the stock market is the only place we know of where people get more interested when the prices are being raised. They seem to lose interest when stocks are "on sale."

Where does that leave you, if you'll never know when it's the best time to invest? Actually in a very good place. Armchair Millionaires understand that while the market can't be predicted in the short term, it does go up over the long term. And so the best thing to do with your long-term savings is to invest in the stock market all the time. Because stock markets, while having bad days—even bad years—tend to go up over time.

So resolve yourself right now to never knowing the absolute best time to invest in the stock market.

Yet you do know that you want to earn that 11 percent return (like your grandfather did) by being invested in the stock market. So when should you invest? All the time! Meaning that each month, you should invest the same amount of money in stocks. No worrying, no wondering, just the same old boring investment every month.

This approach to investing is called "dollar cost averaging." When you put dollar cost averaging to work in your financial plan, you invest all the money you're saving each month into the stock market, no matter how high or low the market is. (Remember, we'll cover the question, "What should you invest in?" in Chapter 8.)

When you invest a set amount each month—say $90—your money will buy you fewer shares when the market is high, and more shares when it's low. You'll put dollar cost averaging to work and sleep well every night, knowing that, over time, you're buying the number of shares that's just right for your budget.

	Monthly Investment	Share Price	Number of Shares	Cumulative Cost	Total Worth of Investment
Month 1	EACH MONTH YOU INVEST **$90**	$9	10	$90	$90
Month 2	$90	**$3** OUCH! BIG DROP!	30	$180	$120
Month 3	$90	$6	15	**$270**	**$330** WOW! A PROFIT!

The reason dollar cost averaging works is that it forces you to buy fewer shares when the stock market is high and more shares when the market is low. You can think of it as automatically buying more shares any time the market is on sale. Plus, since it helps you to "buy low" every time you invest, dollar cost averaging boosts portfolio performance, even when the stock market fluctuates. In time, a regular investment plan like this helps to smooth out the market's ups and downs. The bonus is that this strategy boosts your return over time, and takes away your day-to-day worries about the normal swings in the market.

Dollar cost averaging is easy to understand, even easier to do, and the long-term effect it will have on your portfolio will bring tears (of joy!) to your eyes. To quote John Bogle, one of Wall Street's most successful money managers, "As far as investing is concerned, dollar cost averaging suggests that slow-and-steady will likely win the race."

Does It Work?

Sure, it sounds great in theory, but does it really work?

A lot of it depends on whether you can stomach the market's ups and downs. Even though time is on your side, there may be months—even years—when your investments will be worth less than you paid. This can test the mettle of the most knowledgeable investor. Tools like dollar cost averaging can protect you, but only if you're ready to stick to a plan in good times and bad.

Imagine this: You return from vacation, log on to your computer and discover that the market has crashed and your $10,000 portfolio is now worth $5,000. Do you sell? Or do you keep buying every month using dollar cost averaging?

a. Sell it all
b. Stick to the plan

Armchair Millionaires know that it's best not to panic when the market falls. In fact, dollar cost averaging can be your friend in declining markets if you stick to the plan.

Dollar Cost Averaging in Retrospect

To really see how dollar cost averaging works, we have to go back in time a bit. Let's compare how it would have worked with your investment during the worst bear market in history—the Great Depression.

Assume for a minute that you started investing near the beginning of the Depression. If you had made a lump sum investment on January 1, 1928, you would have *lost* an average of 0.9 percent every year through 1938 (ouch!). On the other hand, with regular monthly investments throughout the Depression, your average annual *gain* would have been 7.4 percent.

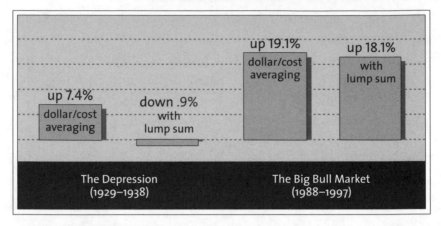

Regular Investing Is a Winner in
Bull and Bear Markets

But dollar cost averaging also works in rising markets. Consider the greatest bull market in history—1988 through 1997. If you had invested a lump sum on January 1, 1988, your average yearly return through the end of 1997 would have been 18.1 percent. Regular monthly investments made during that same time would have returned you an average of 19.1 percent.

(This calculation assumes that your savings were invested in the stock market in the S&P 500 index. It also assumes that you reinvested all your interest, dividends, and capital gains.)

As you can see, dollar cost averaging really helps you maximize your return during the down markets, but still lets you enjoy the great returns of bull markets. Over time, it can make a huge difference in your portfolio's value.

If you've ever asked yourself, "Is this the right time to get into the stock market?" or said, "The market's too high now. I've missed my chance," you'll soon forget those words after you've learned about the power of dollar cost averaging every month.

Investing in the stock market regularly gives your money the force of a one-two punch: You have the best long-term investment, along with a powerful tool—dollar cost averaging—that will bolster the worth of your investment during good and bad markets.

Perhaps the Best Part of Dollar Cost Averaging—Peace of Mind

Another very powerful aspect of dollar cost averaging is its ability to let you relax. No matter what happens in the market, or how you're feeling about your finances, dollar cost averaging insures that your investment plan keeps marching on undisturbed. And this positive impact on your emotional health is what makes the Armchair Millionaire plan so livable, and so successful. Because if you become stressed out over a dip in the market, you could panic and sell your shares when prices are low (and all Armchair Millionaires know that is a quick way to lose money). With dollar cost averaging in the arsenal of investment tools, Armchair Millionaires have the emotional security of being able to keep their wits about them no matter what's happening in the market. Here, some Armchair Millionaire members explain exactly how investing on a regular schedule helps them sleep at night.

The Long-Term Payoffs

"One of the best reasons for dollar cost averaging is that, over time, you'll pay less for your fund shares than if you'd bought in big blocks every year or so. You get the peace of mind knowing that you're ensuring a good return over the long term without ever trying to time the market (which is nearly impossible for even the experts to do consistently)."

—Armchair Millionaire member bandl

No More Waiting for Lady Luck

"Think about it this way: Each year, you set aside $1,000 to buy shares of mutual fund X. You decide to wait and watch until the shares are as low as you think they'll go. If you did this, you would be trying to time the market. And timing the market is not the kind of thing an amateur can do. Frankly, I'm skeptical that even the pros can do it. If you know someone who has timed the market and made a lot of money that way, don't be seduced. They were lucky. I don't like luck being a part of my investing strategy. That's why I go to Vegas."

—Armchair Millionaire member Rose

The Bigger Picture

"Here's why dollar cost averaging and indexing are so smart. They don't assume any single narrow investing strategy will be the one and only one that works. Instead, dollar cost averaging takes a really broad view of the markets and merely predicts that the markets will continue, on average, to rise in the future. It's hard to dispute the evidence of more than a century's worth of stock market data. People have to understand what risk is and not just turn away some good ideas because there is an element of risk. Not investing intelligently is the biggest risk of all."

—Armchair Millionaire member Matt

From the Armchair Millionaire's Gallery—
Meet Armchair Millionaire Member AMDave, Dollar Cost Averager Extraordinaire

AMDave is an official community leader for the Armchair Millionaire Web site. Dave's exuberance for the Armchair Millionaire plan and his ability to encourage conversation make him a natural at helping everyday folks start their investment plan. Here, Dave explains how he got started investing, and why dollar cost averaging is such an important part of his financial plan.

Armchair Millionaire Member Name: AMDave
From: Horsham, Pennsylvania
Age: 33
Occupation: Networking Consultant
Family Status: Married, with daughter (17 months) and another child on the way

Financial goal: Retirement, college for children
How far along are you? On track so far

What was your biggest misconception before you started investing?
I used to think that investing in the stock market was no different from going to the casino. I still believe that's true in the short term. In the long term however, the market eventually works its way upward, making it a good place to put money (on a regularly timed basis) that won't be needed for several years.

How does dollar cost averaging help you achieve your goal?
By having equal 401(k) plan contributions automatically deducted from my paychecks each month, I buy more shares when the price is low, fewer shares when the price is high. Rather than being upset during the summer of 1998 market correction, I was enjoying buying a greater number of fund shares "on sale" with each payroll deduction. I also don't have to worry about investing a large lump sum just before a market crash, or about procrastinating because of that fear.

What do you want the world to know about investing?
Invest as much as you can as early as you can. Make periodic (preferably automatic) investing part of your life early on, and you'll have a good chance at meeting your financial goals.

Making Dollar Cost Averaging Work for You

Once you've decided on how much you will "Pay Yourself First," you can use that amount to dollar cost average into the stock market. In Chapter 8, you'll learn exactly how to invest in the stock market in order to maximize your returns and minimize your risks.

But instead of writing a check each month, there's an even easier way to put dollar cost averaging to work. You should set up an

Automatic Investment Plan (AIP), which will withdraw that money from your checking account and invest it automatically.

Nearly all brokers and mutual funds offer an AIP option. Why not? It's a great way to make sure their customers keep sending them money. In fact, brokers and financial institutions like AIPs so much they don't even charge for the service.

Beware of Hidden Fees

While dollar cost averaging can make the most of your money, if your account or your chosen investment requires a transaction fee, dollar cost averaging won't be nearly as effective. Below are some words of wisdom from Armchair Millionaires on this topic:

Buyer Beware

"You definitely don't want to get into a relationship with a broker or a mutual fund company that charges you a fee for each automatic investment as if it's a stock transaction. You need to find plans and companies that let you make your automatic investments for free or for annual account charges. In other words, if you dollar cost average $100 a month, don't pay a $25 or $30 transaction fee each time. That would be crazy. If the investment you want to buy can only be bought for a transaction fee, then you might want to consider making one large investment once a year, rather than each month. (Or you might want to change brokers.)"

—Armchair Millionaire member Jes

"I agree. If you think taxes retard your investment's growth, stock transaction fees are deadly. Don't even think about dollar cost averaging if you are paying stock transaction fees every time."

—Armchair Millionaire member Marty

At some brokerages, you'll have to complete two sets of forms, one to authorize the transfer of money each month, and the other to authorize the monthly investment in your chosen mutual fund or other security.

To sign up, request forms for the company's automatic investment plan. You'll probably have to send a cancelled check from your bank account along with the form, and you may need your bank's routing number, but your bank's customer service desk can tell you that in a jiffy.

The beauty of an automatic plan like this is that you'll never have to worry about whether the market is high or low—and you'll never have to put investing on your list of "Things to Do." Your plan will run itself.

In good times or bad, dollar cost averaging is the smartest way to build a portfolio's value for long-term investing. Historically, stock market investments have done better than any other kind of investment over a long time. It's only when you stick with stocks through good and bad that you can earn that 11 percent annual return.

That brings us right up to the third part of our investing decision, "What should I invest in?" Keep on going to Chapter 8 for the answer.

Chapter 7 Action Items

- Determine the fixed amount of money you want to invest each month.
- Open an account at a brokerage firm or mutual fund company, one that has an option to receive automatic payments from your bank account.
- Fill out your AIP forms and send them to the financial institution where you've chosen to open your monthly savings account.

STEP 4:
Use the Armchair
Investing Strategy

So far, we've examined the first two parts of the investing process, knowing 1) where to invest (in the stock market) and 2) when to invest (always, so you can take advantage of dollar cost averaging). For many people, the toughest part about investing is the last part of the equation: 3. **What should you invest in?**

Knowing that the stock market is where you *need* to be regularly investing if you want to become an Armchair Millionaire isn't enough. How do you analyze investments? What stocks or mutual funds should you buy? And when should you sell?

Many Wall Street professionals have spent millions of dollars testing various theories on which stocks to buy and how long to hold them. Fortunately for you, the Armchair Millionaire has developed a simple, yet highly effective approach to long-term investing in the stock market. It incorporates decades of academic research done at some of the greatest universities, as well as some ideas from the sharpest investing minds of all time.

We call our program the Armchair Investing Strategy. While it includes investing methods that have been around, and have been used successfully for years, they have never been brought together into one comprehensive strategy. What's more, you can put the plan to work at lots of brokerage firms and mutual fund companies without having to pay lots of fees or commissions. It's elementary enough so you won't need an MBA or a degree in accounting in order to put it to work. And it won't require that you spend hours a day (or hours a week—or even hours a month) managing your portfolio once you've got it up and running. For people with busy lives, the Armchair Investing Strategy is a way to invest without giving up your hobbies or family time.

Part A—Why the Armchair Investing Strategy Works

For most investors, the Armchair Investing Strategy will be the perfect way to make your money work for you over the long term. But the fact that the Armchair Investing Strategy is near-Nirvana didn't happen by accident. When we developed this approach to the stock market, we started out by studying what all the experts had to say about what works, and looked for a strategy that meets eight basic criteria.

Eight Criteria for a Near-Perfect Investing Strategy

1. THE STRATEGY MUST BE EASY TO START. We looked for an investing method that anyone could implement quite simply, with any amount of money, from $50 to $50,000.

2. THE STRATEGY MUST BE EASY TO MAINTAIN. Once you're up and running with your portfolio, it shouldn't require hours of work each day, or each week, or even each month. You shouldn't need to spend all your free time researching stocks and mutual funds, or spending hours on the phone with your broker, or reading the stock tables in the newspaper, or doing calculations in a spreadsheet.

3. THE STRATEGY MUST BE EASY TO UNDERSTAND. What good are complicated investing strategies that require you to wade through financial textbooks or to go back to college for an advanced degree? "Easy to understand" doesn't mean "unsophisticated," however.

4. THE STRATEGY MUST BE INEXPENSIVE TO IMPLEMENT AND TO MAINTAIN. In this instance, we're not talking about the amount of money that you actually invest—we're referring to the fees, commissions, and expenses some investment plans require that can add up to a small fortune over the years. In fact, one of the two biggest factors that can kill long-term gains in a portfolio is the cost of management. Investors who are consistently trading stocks and funds, buying and selling on a daily or weekly basis, risk watching their returns become seriously reduced by the amount they pay in commissions (not to mention the taxes on all those short-term gains). If you have to pay hundreds of dollars for data and reports and subscriptions, then all these expenses will also reduce your returns.

5. THE STRATEGY MUST BE TAX-EFFICIENT. Taxes are the other item that can put a big dent in the long-term gains in a portfolio. Whenever you have profits in your portfolio, either from dividends, interest, or capital gains (when you sell a stock or mutual fund), you'll have to pay taxes to the IRS. What's worse is that frequent traders have to pay higher taxes, since gains on stocks you've owned for less than a year don't receive the lower capital gains tax rate of 20 percent. Instead, short-term capital gains are taxed at your ordinary income rate—if you're in the 28 percent tax bracket, you'll pay taxes of 28 percent on your short-term earnings. If you want to be a millionaire, you'll definitely want to pay less in taxes over the years.

6. THE STRATEGY MUST BE WIDELY AVAILABLE. What good is an investing plan that you can't use in your 401(k), or with the broker of your choice? The Armchair Investing Strategy can be used in some form or other at just about any mutual fund company or brokerage firm in the country.

7. THE STRATEGY MUST HAVE A LOT OF HISTORY TO JUDGE IT BY. If you're investing for the long term, you'll want a plan that's been proven over the long term. At the end of the twentieth century, the U.S. stock market was in one of the biggest bull markets in its history. In the 1990s, the stock market grew tremendously, and most investors will barely remember the minor blips in 1997 and 1998 (as they will likely forget the turbulence in the spring of 2000). But things won't always look so rosy, if history is our guide. A lot of mutual funds and investment advisors advertise great track records over the past five years, but anyone can look like an investing genius in a bull market. When the market turns south, and experiences a few years of declining returns, how will those portfolios perform?

Instead, we looked for a strategy that has worked well through bull and bear markets, going back to at least 1970. Why 1970? Well, the U.S. stock market had one of its worst bear markets in the 1970s, so evaluating a portfolio based on its performance since then can give us a good idea how it will likely perform in the next bear market.

8. FINALLY, THE STRATEGY MUST MAKE A LOT OF MONEY (NATURALLY!). After all, who wants an easy, understandable, inexpensive, tax-efficient, widely available investing plan with a long history if it doesn't generate a good rate of return? And the winner is . . .

There's only one way to invest in the stock market that meets all those criteria—and it's called "Indexing." Indexing is a way of investing so that you match the returns of an entire stock market index, guaranteed. An indexed portfolio provides every single one of the advantages outlined above.

In fact, one of the finest investors of our time, Warren Buffet, says that indexing is the best approach to the stock market for 99 percent of all investors. But before we can tell you why indexing is so great, we first have to take a detailed look at what indexing is. Bear with us—there's a lot of information to go over, but we promise it all fits into one cohesive, easy-to-understand package. Honest.

What Is a Market Index?

In order to understand the Armchair Investing Strategy, you must first know what a stock market index is. You've probably heard of one of the most common stock market indexes, the Dow Jones Industrial Average (also known as "the Dow" or the "Dow 30"). The Dow is a collection of thirty stocks that represent some of the biggest companies in American business. Every day, the prices of all thirty stocks are used to determine the value of the Dow Jones Industrial Average. Investors look at the value of the Dow and use it as a gauge of the entire market—if the Dow is up, the market as a whole is usually up. If the Dow is down, the rest of the market is usually down as well.

Another common index is the Standard & Poor's 500. The S&P 500 includes five hundred companies of all sizes and from all industries, chosen by S&P to represent the full spectrum of American business. It includes computer companies, utilities, transportation companies, manufacturers, restaurants, stores—you name the industry and it's probably represented by the S&P 500. While the S&P 500 contains small and large companies, the largest companies dominate the index because it's weighted by market capitalization. That means that S&P first considers the size of a company relative to other companies (in financial speak, this is known as a company's "market capitalization" or "market cap"). Then, it adds enough of that company's shares to the S&P 500 so that it is represented in the index in the same proportion. Or, to put it more simply, bigger companies have more shares in the index than do smaller companies.

The Dow 30 and the S&P 500 aren't the only indexes of the stock market. There are indexes that range from the obvious (such as the Dow or S&P 500) to the obscure (such as the Bloomberg Football Club Index, which represents the performance of publicly traded

British soccer teams). There are indexes that track the performance of particular industries and of the stocks in particular countries. There are indexes for small companies, large companies, and those in between.

Investors and mutual fund managers like to measure their own results against the performance of a particular index. For instance, a mutual fund that invests in large companies might use the S&P 500 as a benchmark by which they can let the world know just how well they're doing.

What Is a Mutual Fund?

Mutual funds are one of the most popular investments available. A mutual fund is a pool of money that's been contributed by investors, is actively maintained by a manager (a single person or a team of investment analysts who invest all the contributions of investors in a single portfolio), and is invested in companies the manager hand-selects. A mutual fund can hold stocks, or bonds, or cash, or other assets, and there are funds that are devoted to specific investing strategies, countries, or regions of the world. Among stock funds, there are those that invest in technology stocks and those that invest in utility stocks and so on. No matter what your financial flavor is, chances are there are funds that fit the bill.

The main advantages of mutual funds are that your money is managed by professionals, you can easily build a diversified portfolio, and you can invest relatively small amounts without paying a lot in fees and commissions.

ADVICE FROM RICH

A lot of investors like to invest in stocks directly, without going through a mutual fund. Although the Armchair Investing Strategy is based on investing in mutual funds, it doesn't mean you have to give up your stock-picking habit entirely. Many Armchair Millionaires use what's called the "core and explore" method of building a portfolio.

> They use the Armchair Investing Strategy for their "core" portfolio, investing at least half of their total assets using our approach. Then they use the other portion of their portfolio to "explore" the world of stocks and other investments.

Standard mutual funds aren't all peaches and cream, though. One of the main disadvantages to mutual funds is that they often charge fees to offset the cost of the manager's salary. Along the same lines, because managers are directly responsible for a fund's performance, they can quickly change the makeup of a mutual fund to boost earnings (or cut losses), meaning that the fund you buy into isn't necessarily the fund you'll end up with at any given point in time. And finally, even if you find a mutual fund with a manager whose track record you respect, that manager may leave, again opening you up to the possibility that the fund you buy into won't be the same one you end up with.

The Beauty of an Index Fund

An index fund allows you to enjoy the good parts of a mutual fund with little of the bad by buying stock in all the companies of a particular index. That's how an index fund can reproduce the performance of an entire section of the market. An index fund builds its portfolio by simply buying all of the stocks in a particular index—in effect, buying the entire stock market, not just a few stocks. The most popular index of stock index funds is the Standard & Poor's 500. There are index funds that track twenty-eight different indexes, and more are added all the time.

An S&P 500 stock index fund owns five hundred stocks—all of the companies that are included in the index. This is the key distinction between stock index funds and "actively managed" mutual funds. The manager of a stock index fund doesn't have to worry about which stocks to buy or sell—he or she only has to buy the stocks that are included in the fund's chosen index. A stock index fund has no need for a team of highly paid stock analysts and expensive computer equipment to pick stocks for the fund's portfolio. So the hardest part of running a mutual fund is eliminated.

That's great because an index mutual fund is much cheaper to run than an active fund. Eliminate those analysts' salaries and an index fund can cut its costs tremendously. Those savings can be passed along to investors in the form of higher returns. Remember, reducing commissions is an easy and powerful way to boost your investing returns.

ADVICE FROM RICH

The average time that an index used in the Armchair Investing Strategy has existed is 35.3 years. This is good news for people who believe that the more information you have, the more intelligent decisions you can make. Investors in index funds are more comfortable investing with the benefit of decades of information.

Since index funds diversify by buying all the companies in an index rather than by trying to pick winners and losers, they aren't going to "beat the market." But they're guaranteed not to underperform their benchmark index either (at least by a significant margin).

If that sounds like a plan that guarantees mediocrity, it is—and that's good!

You see, the main advantage of stock index funds is that they perform better than actively managed funds. Some investors find it incredible when they learn that most mutual funds are flops, at least when it comes to generating returns for their shareholders. From 1995 to 1999, for instance, nearly 85 percent of all mutual funds that were set up to beat the S&P 500 failed to meet that goal in any particular year. When you think about it, that's an incredible statistic—8 out of 10 mutual funds can't beat the market. If the investors in those funds only knew what Armchair Millionaires know, they'd be much better off. Investing in an index fund guarantees that you'll always match the performance of the overall market.

EXTRA! EXTRA! Read all about it! Index Funds Clobber Actively Managed Funds

Sure, investing in a stock index fund also guarantees that you'll never outperform the overall market, but fewer than 20 percent of all professional mutual fund managers can reach that goal in any given year. Even armed with this knowledge, some investors are convinced they can pick out one of the funds that will be in the rare 20 percent club. Armchair Millionaires, though, know that this sounds easy in theory but is actually much harder in practice. If you look at a list of the top-performing mutual funds for the last several years, you won't likely find many of the same names on more than a few lists. It's not uncommon for a fund to have a "hot" year, but it's very uncommon for a fund to consistently turn in above-average performance.

Back in Chapter 7, you learned how the stock market has generated better returns than just about any other kind of investment. When you invest in stock index funds, you get the same kinds of returns as the whole market in your own portfolio. And when you consider the failure rate of active funds, being doomed to an "average" performance in your portfolio doesn't seem like such a bad deal, does it?

Modern Portfolio Theory—A Fancy Way of Saying "Minimize Risk, Maximize Returns"

By now, you've probably guessed that the Armchair Investing Strategy uses index funds as its primary investment vehicle. But you don't have to take our word on the benefits of passive investing through the use of index funds. The Armchair Investment Strategy is really an extension of a well-respected school of thought called the "Modern Portfolio Theory."

The Modern Portfolio Theory was first developed by an economics student named Harry Markowitz in the early 1950s. Working on his doctoral thesis at the University of Chicago, Markowitz figured out that it is possible to build a portfolio that will generate above-average returns but with below-average risk. That's good news for Armchair Millionaires.

Markowitz defined risk as going hand-in-hand with returns in an investment portfolio. Investors always like to reduce the risk of their stocks falling drastically in price, but rather than worry about the risk level of individual stocks, Markowitz suggested that investors look at the risk of their overall portfolio.

ADVICE FROM RICH

One of the basic concepts of the Armchair Millionaire approach to investing is the "asset class." We've discussed asset classes before, but it bears repeating. An asset class is a way experts group different types of investments that share common characteristics. For instance, all of the following are asset classes: real estate, precious metals (gold, silver), stocks, bonds, cash. Making the decision about how much of your portfolio to invest in any of these asset classes is known as "asset allocation" or "asset class investing."

HOW DO YOU FIGURE OUT THE RISKS IN A STOCK OR PORTFOLIO? Markowitz says that you should look at how the different stocks or different "asset classes" move in price relative to one another. For instance, the stock of an umbrella manufacturer and the stock of a suntan lotion company are both dependent on the overall climate. And while a rainy season is a blessing for the umbrella manufacturer, it's a curse for the suntan lotion business. In academic terms, these two companies have a low "correlation." If you own either stock in your portfolio, you might expect wild swings in their share prices depending on the weather—a high-risk proposition.

But what if you owned both stocks? Then, no matter whether the sun shone or the clouds poured, your portfolio would have one stock that would be doing well. This reduces the risks in your overall portfolio. The good news, according to Markowitz, is that these two companies don't entirely cancel each other out. By adding more and more companies to your portfolio, you can decrease the risk and increase your returns.

Armchair Millionaires know that when you put all this together, it's entirely possible to build a portfolio that has a much higher average return than the level of risk it contains. When you build a diversified portfolio and spread out your investments among stocks that have a low correlation, you're really just managing risk and return. That's not so complicated, is it? Well, it was pretty radical for Wall Street back in the 1950s, and it took some time for Modern Portfolio Theory to take hold in the minds of professional investment managers. By 1990, Modern Portfolio Theory was considered so important to investing that Markowitz received the Nobel Prize for Economics.

The Efficient Market Hypothesis, or Why Picking Individual Stocks Doesn't Work

Building on Markowitz's work, a researcher named Eugene Fama developed a theory about the market in the 1960s that claimed it was impossible to pick individual stocks that were undervalued or overvalued at any particular time. Fama explained that at any point in time, the prices of all stocks reflect all the available information about those stocks. Since the prices of stocks are always "correct," it's fruitless to try to pick individual stocks that you think will go up in price—any future price movements are due to factors that you can't predict.

Fama's theory is called the "Efficient Market Hypothesis," and it was a pretty radical idea for the scores of investment analysts who make their living by telling clients what stocks to buy and sell. Unlike buying a car, where you can negotiate a price that's better than the sticker price, you can't buy stocks at a near-wholesale price. Since the stock market prices a stock "efficiently," you'll never be able to get a bargain when you try to buy individual stocks.

What's more, Fama demonstrated how price movements of individual stocks do not follow any trends or patterns at all. Past price movements cannot be used to predict future prices—stock prices always move randomly. This is known as the "Random Walk Theory," named after the zigzagging path a drunk might make as he walks down the sidewalk. (Burton Malkiel popularized the Random Walk Theory in his classic book, *A Random Walk Down Wall Street.*) All this academic research points to just one conclusion: It's impossible to build a portfolio based on individual stock picking, if you want to reduce your risk and still maintain a decent return.

The Armchair Investing Strategy—Many Investing Theories Distilled into One

So how do you invest? The answer is clear—instead of picking stocks, you should invest in an entire stock market. That way, you'll get the benefits of diversification and noncorrelating markets and asset classes, and you won't sidetrack your portfolio by making mistakes in the stocks you pick. And you can invest in the entire stock market by investing in a stock market index fund.

Institutional investors, often referred to as "smart money," have always favored an indexing approach to their portfolios. These managers of pension funds and other large investment portfolios put an average of 40 percent of their assets into index funds. Individual investors, however, are just catching on, and only invest 5 percent of their assets in index funds. But since individuals are putting $10 of every $15 they put in mutual funds into index funds, some experts foresee that individuals could have 50 percent of their assets in index funds within the next decade, finally catching up to the "smart money."

Part B—The Nuts and Bolts of the Armchair Investing Strategy

As you can see, investing in index funds is a smart choice for most investors. The next component is to determine which indexes you should invest in—or, to put it another way, which sub-asset classes you should invest in.

Remember that asset classes are the major categories of investments that you can make in a portfolio. Stocks, bonds, cash, real estate, and precious metals are examples of assets that you can own as an investor. The Armchair Investing Strategy aims to invest primarily in a single asset class—the stock market. It is the stock market alone that has grown the fastest over this century.

Investment Returns: Stocks, Bonds, & Bills: 1926–2000*

Asset Class	Average Annual Total Return
Stocks (S&P 500 Index)	+11.2%
Bonds (Long-Term U.S. Government)	+5.2%
Cash (U.S. Treasury bills)	+3.8%

*As of June 30, 2000

But just knowing that you want to invest 100 percent of your portfolio in the stock market isn't very specific. You need to get more targeted than just picking an asset class. You need to pick a sub-asset class. For instance, should you buy U.S. stocks or stocks from other countries? Large companies or small companies? These are all sub-asset classes, and deciding which of these groups you want to invest in and how much you should invest in the selected groups is the key to the Armchair Investing Strategy.

How Does the Armchair Investing Strategy Work?

Once you've settled on the concept of investing in index funds (a historically superior choice, Armchair Millionaires believe), your next step is to find the right mix of funds that will help you meet your goal of becoming a millionaire without the slightest risk of becoming a pauper in the interim.

The Armchair Investing Strategy requires that you invest your portfolio in index funds that track the indexes of three sub-asset classes:

- One that invests in large companies in the U.S.
- One that invests in small companies in the U.S.
- One that invests in large companies outside the U.S.

Bigger and Better: The S&P 500

The first mutual fund in the Armchair Investing Strategy is any mutual fund that mimics the Standard and Poor's 500 Stock Index (also known as the S&P 500).

Here is a list of some of the index funds that follow the S&P 500:

Advantus Index 500 Fund A (ADIAX)

Aetna Index Plus Large Cap A (AELAX)

Aon S&P 500 Index (ASPYX)

California Investment Trust S&P 500 Index (SPFIX)

Dreyfus S&P 500 Index (PEOPX)

E*Trade S&P 500 Index (ETSPX)

Evergreen Select Equity Index A (ESINX)

Fidelity Spartan Market Index (FSMKX)

First American-Equity Index A (FAEIX)

Galaxy II Large Co. Index (ILCIX)

Harris Insight Trust Index (HIDAX)

Invesco S& P 500 Index (ISPIX)

Kent Index Equity (KNIDX)

MainStay Equity Index A (MCSEX)

Munder Index 500 A (MUXAX)

Northern Stock Index (NOSIX)

One Group-Equity Index A (OGEAX)

PIMCO Stocks PLUS Fund A (PSPAX)

Schwab S&P 500 Index (SWPIX)

Scudder S&P 500 Index (SCPIX)

State Street Global Advisors S&P 500 Index (SVSPX)

Strong Index 500 (SINEX)

T. Rowe Price Equity Index (PREIX)

Transamerica Premier Index (TPIIX)

USAA S&P 500 Index (USSPX)

Vanguard Index Trust 500 (VFINX)

Wachovia Equity Index A (BTEIX)

Wells Fargo Equity Index A (SFCSX)

(You can find complete contact information for these funds in Appendix B.)

The S&P 500 is a collection of 500 of the biggest and best companies in America. The stocks in the S&P 500 are determined by the S&P's Index Committee, who choose companies that can serve as a proxy of American business.

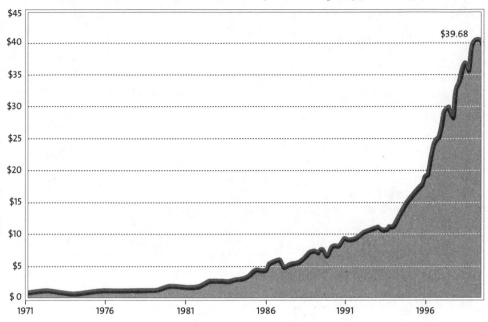

Growth of $1.00 Invested in the S&P 500, January 1, 1972–June 30, 2000

Most of the companies in the S&P 500 are quite big, so their stocks are known as "large-cap" (large-capitalization) stocks. The companies in the S&P 500 range from GE (the largest company in America, worth more than $572.3 billion) to the five-hundredth company, Owens Corning (a building materials manufacturer with a value of $277.4 million). It is safe to say that if America is doing well, you can tell it from the rise in the S&P 500. And if America is doing poorly, so is the S&P 500.

Even though the Dow Jones Industrial Average is the "index" most widely reported to the public, it is the S&P 500 that is the most widely followed by professional investors. If you had invested $1,000 in the S&P 500 at the end of 1925, it would be worth $3 million at the end of 1999! Since 1972, the S&P 500 has gone up an average of 13.79 percent annually.

Small Is Good, Too

The second mutual fund in the Armchair Investing Strategy is one that mimics the popular index called "The Russell 2000."

These mutual funds follow the Russell 2000 or other small-cap index:

> AXP Small Company Index A (ISIAX)
> Federated Mini-Cap C (MNCCX)
> Fund Information
> Galaxy II Small Company Index (ISCIX)
> Gateway Small Cap Index (GSCIX)
> Merrill Lynch Small Cap Index D (MDSKX)
> Schwab Small Cap Index (SWSMX)
> Vanguard Index Trust Small Cap (NAESX)

(You can find complete contact information for these funds in Appendix B.)

The Russell 2000 is a proxy of small businesses in America, and is maintained by the Frank Russell Company. Historically, small businesses grow faster than the big ones. This makes sense. It takes a lot to radically affect the business of the biggest companies, whereas sometimes the future prospects of a small company can be impacted, positively or negatively, by one new client or a single business opportunity.

This brings us to our next point. The small companies (we call them "small-cap stocks") in the Russell 2000 tend to go up and down a lot more (this is known as volatility) than do the biggest companies. That's why it makes sense to diversify, by buying an index of all the small companies in America. This index will incorporate the good news and the bad news into one big picture, providing an average performance experienced by all of the small companies in the index.

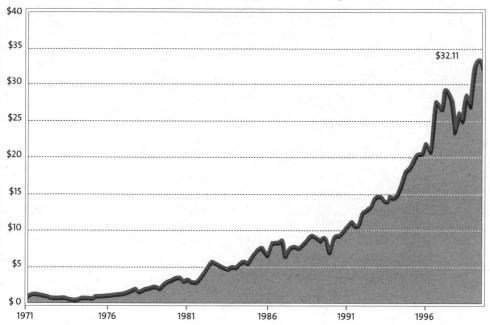

Growth of $1.00 Invested in the Russell 2000, January 1, 1972–June 30, 2000

Since 1972, small-cap stocks, as represented by the Russell 2000, have returned an average annual gain of 12.94 percent.

Going Global with EAFE

An idea as good as the Armchair Investing Strategy only gets better. The third and final mutual fund in our plan follows another index fund, Morgan Stanley's Europe, Australasia, Far East Index, often referred to as the EAFE index and pronounced "eefah."

These mutual funds follow the EAFE Index:

Dreyfus International Stock Index (DIISX)

E*Trade International Index (ETINX)

First American International Index A (FIIAX)

First American International Index B (FIXBX)

Merrill Lynch International Index D (MDIIX)

One Group Intl Equity Index A (OEIAX)

One Group Intl Equity Index B (OGEBX)

One Group Intl Equity Index C (OIICX)

Schwab International Index (SWINX)

Vanguard Total Intl Stock Index (VGTSX)

(You can find complete contact information for these funds in Appendix B.)

The EAFE Index mimics the performance of publicly traded stocks around the world, with the exception of the United States.

Investing internationally has gotten a bad rap in the last decade because the strength of America's economy has left so many other countries in the dust. But this wasn't always so. From 1983 through 1988, the Morgan Stanley EAFE Index easily outperformed the S&P 500 each year.

Growth of $1.00 Invested in EAFE January 1, 1972–June 30, 2000

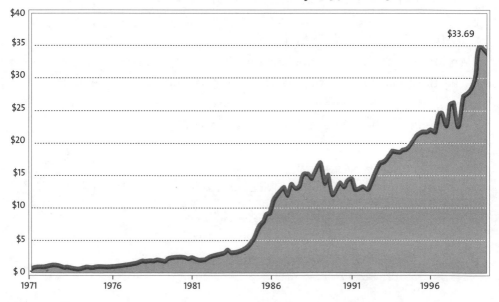

If you're investing for the long haul, it makes sense to participate in growth all over the world, not just in your own country. And don't even think of trying to figure out when the right moment is to invest internationally. That's called "market timing" and it's a sucker's game. Even if you get it right, it's probably more due to luck than to brains. The average annual return of the EAFE index has been 13.14 percent since 1972.

Why Does the Armchair Investing Strategy Work?

There are three very good reasons for the Armchair Investing Strategy's success.

First, it's important to note that the Armchair Investing Strategy invests entirely in the stock market. Over the past fifty years, not only have equities outperformed the government bond market, but they have also easily outpaced inflation, which is the minimum standard of performance for all investors. If you want to become a millionaire, you need to be invested in the stock market. Each of the index funds in our strategy invests solely in stocks.

Second, index funds provide broad diversification at a very reasonable price. Rather than trying to pick winners and losers in the stock market (usually a fruitless endeavor), an index fund invests in an entire market, and therefore always matches the benchmark it seeks to beat. Financial experts tell us that no matter the time frame, as much as 90 percent of the success of the Armchair Millionaire portfolio comes from picking the right asset class for the job. The other 10 percent will come from investing at the right time and choosing the right individual investments. In other words, while most people spend their energy looking for the next Microsoft and worrying about the next market top, the largest part of your long-term portfolio's return will come from just choosing the stock market as your investing vehicle of choice.

It is true that some people can pick the winners in any market some of the time, but it is rare that anyone can do it all of the time. It's so rare, in fact, that in the ten-year period ending in mid-1995, the S&P 500 Index beat 83 percent of all actively-managed general stock mutual funds. That's where diversification comes in—by spreading your money around several different sub-asset classes, you can always make sure you've got the big winner in your portfolio.

Perhaps the Best Part of the Armchair Investing Strategy

Throughout this book, we've been telling you that the Armchair Millionaire plan is great not only because it can make you rich, but because it can actually take a load off your mind. We're not going to say it again here. Instead, we're going to let one of our members say it for us.

Running on Auto-Pilot

"I have learned to pretty much leave my portfolio alone. It seems I was always tweaking it and trying to figure out a good investment strategy, racking up a lot of commissions and headaches for myself in the process. I've since learned an excellent and easy strategy since coming to the Armchair Millionaire site. I have my automatic exchanges set up for all my investment accounts and now all I need to do is watch my money grow."

—Armchair Millionaire member MarcusJN

Third, the Armchair Investing Strategy benefits from the advantages of a long-term perspective.

As John Bowen, expert financial advisor, explains, "The minimum expected investment period for any portfolio containing equity securities is five years. This five-year minimum investment period is important in that the investment process must be viewed as a long-term plan for achieving the desired results. This is because one-year volatility can be significant for certain asset classes. However, over a five-year period, volatility is greatly reduced."

Finally, each of these index funds represents a different segment of the stock market. The S&P 500 is representative of the U.S.'s largest companies, while the Russell 2000 includes much smaller companies. Academic research shows that the largest and smallest companies' stocks have a low correlation with each other. In other words, when one of these asset classes is not performing well, the other ones may likely be going strong. This further minimizes the risks associated with volatility.

The EAFE Index represents stocks from Japan, the United Kingdom, Europe, and the Pacific Rim. It's important to invest in these markets because international and U.S. stocks have a low correlation.

"Building a portfolio containing asset classes with low correlation to each other results in greater long-term performance for the investor while reducing risk through diversification," says Bowen.

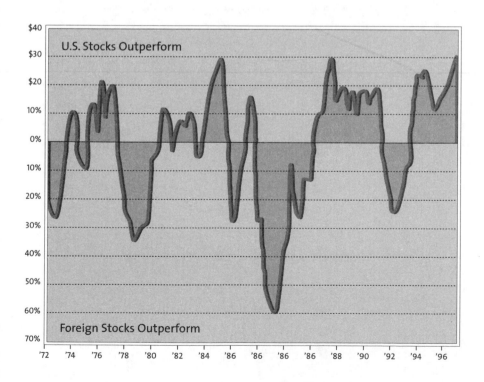

ADVICE FROM RICH

In the graph on page 143, you can see the periods since 1972 when U.S. stocks outperformed foreign stocks (as represented by the S&P 500 and the Morgan Stanley EAFE), and vice versa. If these markets had a close correlation, the peaks and valleys on both sides of the zero percent line would have been fairly close to the line. As you can see, however, these two markets have tended to have big swings in their returns when compared to each other.

Investing using the Armchair Investing Strategy takes advantage of two sets of noncorrelating markets: big U.S. companies versus small U.S. companies, and American companies versus international ones. There's no guarantee that they won't all do badly at the same time, but statistically speaking, it doesn't happen that way very often.

Growth of $1.00 from January 1, 1972–June 30, 2000 in the Armchair Millionaire Strategy

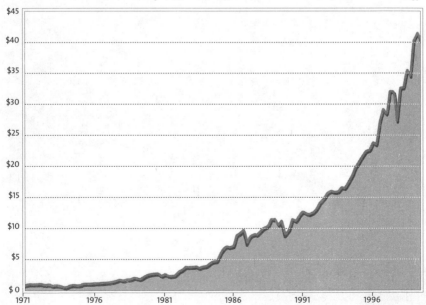

The Numbers Speak for Themselves

If you had invested $1,000 according to the Armchair Investing Strategy back on January 1, 1972, you would have had $35,156 on June 30, 2000. That's an annual rate of return of 13.3 pecent on your initial investment—not bad at all. Imagine what your return would be if you continually put a little money into the Armchair Investing Strategy every month by Paying Yourself First!

ADVICE FROM RICH

As you use the Armchair Investing Strategy, there will doubtless be times when it seems like some hot sector of the market is zooming right by you. Or some friend will boast about the market-besting returns she's gotten in some mutual fund or stock. While it's only human nature to second-guess your investment decisions, it's vital to remember that Armchair Investing is about long-term performance, not short-term profits. Over the long term, the Armchair Investing Strategy works. For a little reality check, the next time a friend brags about his stock-picking skills, ask him to tell you some tales about his losing picks, too.

These results assume an initial investment of $333.33 in the S&P 500, the Russell 2000, and the Morgan Stanley EAFE (in equal thirds) on January 1, 1972, with all subsequently paid dividends reinvested each quarter. The annual returns of each of the indexes in the Model Portfolio for the period are:

Morgan Stanley EAFE: 13.14%
Standard & Poor's 500: 13.79%
Russell 2000: 12.94%

Note: Since the Russell 2000 was created in 1984, and back adjusted to 1979, results are based on DFA 9 & 10 prior to December 1978.

Part C—From the Armchair Millionaire's Gallery—

Founder Lewis Schiff and His Lovely Wife, Lynette, Set Up Their Armchair Investing Plan

As the founder of the Armchair Millionaire, I don't just talk about the Armchair Investing Strategy. My wife, Lynette, and I use the strategy in our real lives—we pay ourselves first, and every month we use dollar cost averaging to purchase shares of three different index funds, just as you've seen in this chapter. Best of all (for you), we post the actual numbers regarding our regular contributions, account balances, and rates of return at www.ArmchairMillionaire.com. We call this the Armchair Millionaire Model Portfolio—it's how we put our money where our mouths are.

If you're sitting there wondering to yourself, "What does an account that actually uses the Armchair Investing Strategy look like, and how do I make mine happen?" this is where it all becomes clear.

What Is the Model Portfolio?

The Model Portfolio takes all the tenets of Armchair Millionaire-style investing and puts them to work. The portfolio follows us as we rebuild our existing portfolio using the Five Steps to Financial Freedom and the Armchair Investing Strategy. Working with John Bowen, the Armchair Millionaire's official portfolio advisor, we figured out a new approach to saving and investing. The Model Portfolio allows you to follow along and eavesdrop on our discussions and see the plan unfold.

First, the Background

Before we get into the nuts and bolts of the portfolio, let's meet the main characters—Lewis and Lynette

He: Born and raised in New York City

Age: 31

Occupation: Executive Producer and Creator, *The Armchair Million-aire.* Previously worked at *Worth* magazine, launched Worth OnLine in 1995.

Investing Background: Started saving and investing at age 21

She: Born in Chicago; has lived in New York City for 13 years

Age: 35

Occupation: Graphic designer for magazine industry

Investing Background: Began saving and investing soon after meeting Lewis in order to impress him

Where They Are Now: Married in Big Sur, CA, in the summer of 1996, Lynette and Lewis then moved into a co-op apartment on New York's Upper West Side. They met at *Worth* magazine, but both left to start their own businesses. They have a yellow Labrador named Homer.

Their Goals: Lynette and Lewis want to get their respective businesses rolling, then they plan to begin a family and raise their kids in the New York area. In the long term, they plan to save and invest for the next twenty years, then move to a coastal summer community and open a café.

Meet John Bowen, Armchair Millionaire Model Portfolio Advisor

John Bowen worked with us to set up our very own Model Portfolio using the Armchair Investment Strategy. He was the CEO of a financial planning company and is the author of *The Prudent Investor's Guide to Beating the Market.* For many years, Bowen dispensed the usual advice to clients about how to invest their dollars, making specific recommendations about stocks, bonds, and mutual funds after developing a full-blown financial analysis for each client. "These analyses can be a great, great benefit to traditional financial planning," explains Bowen, "but quite honestly, many of these financial plans didn't deliver. It was very frustrating."

At the same time, John was teaching Investment Theory at Golden Gate University's Graduate School. A regular part of his curriculum was why financial products that involved active stock picking and market timing just don't improve performance. In fact, taught Bowen, these strategies subtract from the returns that an advisor can achieve for clients.

But one year, a graduate student raised his hand and said "John, I understand what you're teaching. Are you doing it for your clients?"

At that moment, Bowen had an epiphany. "No, I'm not," he admitted. "Professionals who advise individuals don't encourage passive investing because it doesn't cost a lot to implement and requires very little advice from a broker." And thus the transformation of John's financial advisory firm began. For an entire year, John and his partners went without paychecks as he sought counsel from some of the top minds in academia and finance. In the end, they metamorphosed from a traditional financial planning firm to one on the frontier of investment knowledge.

Soon the firm created a network of financial advisors with a uniform investing approach, thus impacting a greater number of retail clients and changing the way investors invest.

John has worked closely with us to make sure that our Model Portfolio follows the simple Armchair Investing Strategy. He has used his twenty years of experience to make our Model Portfolio one that can help anyone—with any amount of money and time—reach, and even exceed, their financial goals using simple, understandable, commonsense strategies.

STEP 1—DEFINING YOUR FINANCIAL OBJECTIVES. In order to come up with an appropriate financial plan, the first step is always to figure out your financial goals—what's important to you about money and what you want for your future. John Bowen sat down with us to discuss these issues and begin building the Model Portfolio.

John: Working with a couple to help them achieve their investment goals is very different from working with an individual. Finding out who is the dominant personality in the financial relationship is important. Often, the longest and most important conversation is about values and finding out the answer to this one question: Why are you trying to build up this money?

Lewis: I can definitely assure you that Lynette and I have different views on money.

Lynette: [Laugh] That's true.

John: Lynette, what's important to you about money?

Lynette: It's important that I always have enough—and there's no real number value. But if something ever happened to my graphic design business, it'd be important to know that there was enough money to survive.

John: What about you, Lewis?

Lewis: Above all, I would like to avoid worrying about money as much as possible.

John: What would it mean to have enough money, so that you wouldn't worry about it anymore?

Lynette: I never really thought about what's going to happen to me in forty years or anything like that. Then three years ago, I started putting money into an IRA. It all started to take shape for me. Prior to that, I think the details of planning a financial future escaped me. I probably wouldn't be in really great shape if I hadn't met Lewie.

Lewis: I was the exact opposite. I started saving and investing when I was twenty-one years old. I've always been an active investor—that was pretty much my hobby. Now it's clear to me that investing successfully is much simpler than I thought it was, but I took a very roundabout route to figure that out.

So Lynette and I come at this from very different angles. She's sort of new to it and is now putting her first financial plan together. And I've been doing this for over ten years, and now I want to redo my entire portfolio to reflect all the things I've learned by researching investment strategies and creating the Armchair Millionaire program.

John: Making a decision about how to invest is easier than most people think. Much of it is determined by the length of time you are investing for. For example, money that's to be used in the immediate future (up until five years from now) should be treated differently from money that won't be needed for a lot longer. In reality, you need to set your time frame, and then we can begin to examine the risks that are appropriate to the lifestyle you are trying to achieve. Let's separate the risks into two parts. The first is the resources that you're going to need in the next few months or next year or so. These have to stay in some form of cash with some rules of thumb about how much cash you should have in reserve.

Lewis: We've already set aside cash in an emergency fund. I think the most common rule of thumb is to have between two and six months' salary available in a savings account, right?

John: Right. The second part is the money that you're ready to set aside for at least five years. You'll be able to put these funds into inexpensive mutual funds using the Armchair Investing Strategy.

STEP 2—ASSESSING YOUR TOLERANCE FOR RISK. Really thinking about how much risk you can tolerate will greatly affect the outcome of your portfolio. If you don't seriously think about how you might react to a dip in the market, you could panic and sell when the market is low. Selling when stock prices are low is deadly to a portfolio. A little soul-searching will help us understand our attitudes toward risk.

John: Lynette, you describe yourself as a little bit more conservative than Lewis, so I'm going to start out with you on this. One of the things we believe strongly is that the stock market tends to grow over the long term. And I have all the reasons and all the data in the world to prove that. However, there are occasional short-term corrections. A good example is the Asian market. Japan had trouble during most of the 1990s.

So, if we look at any money you are going to invest for the next five, ten years, or for the rest of your life, you have to be prepared for setbacks along the way. Emotionally, each of us can handle a different amount of uncertainty. Because you two have a long-term investing horizon—more than twenty years—the effect of compounding returns on your portfolio will be much larger the more risk that you're willing to take. (See Chapter 9, Step #5 of the Five Steps to Financial Freedom, for more on compounding.) It's important to remember that the occasional setbacks in this strategy will be more severe than a portfolio that's not invested entirely in stocks.

Have you ever thought about your tolerance for a short-term setback like that?

Lynette: To be honest, it scares me. But I would certainly try to do it in a smart, comfortable way that was somewhere between minimum and maximum risk.

Lewis: I would also like to raise the issue of the danger of being too conservative. Someone once told me that investing for growth is really about making sure your money grows farther and faster than the shrinking effect that inflation has on your money.

John: That's why we're going to use an investing strategy, the Armchair Investing Strategy, that takes full advantage of the long-term growth of the market, given your discomfort with risk.

Lynette: So, what do we do next?

STEP 3—OPENING AN ACCOUNT AND SETTING UP THE INVESTMENT.

John: Now it's time to transform your portfolio to match everything we've been talking about. It's not so hard to invest intelligently and with common sense. I love the term "Armchair Investing" because it accurately describes how simple it is to implement

Armchair Investing Strategy. What it fails to do is capture the amount of data, academic research, and long-term success that lies behind this basic strategy. Without exception, when I tell people what the Armchair Investing Strategy is, they are underwhelmed. But they become totally satisfied as time goes by.

Lewis: I know that researching your brokerage firm is another vital step in setting up a successful portfolio—also deciding what services you need out of a firm, and what you are willing to pay for them before you shop around.

If the financial industry wants to know why more people don't invest, they should look no further than the process of opening a new brokerage account. There are several different components to starting a saving and investing plan. Looking back, any one of them could have derailed us from getting our plan started.

Lynette: By far the most intimidating and confusing moment was actually getting the plan started.

Lewis: We decided to change our brokerage because we wanted to take advantage of some of the new features and services other brokerages were offering. Since we already had our strategy mapped out (the Armchair Investing Strategy), we wanted to find a brokerage that had access to all of our mutual fund choices and would allow us to make periodic purchases without a fee. Our new broker will allow us to implement the Armchair Investing Strategy using no-load mutual funds. In addition, since we ended up using a broker and not just a mutual funds company, we'll have a wider array of investment choices in the future. Finally, their Web access is fast and easy to use, something that's important to us.

Lynette: We checked out brokers and companies where we can make ongoing, regular investments without transaction fees.

Lewis: Thirty-five pages of application forms later (yes, 35—that's not a misprint), I was ready to transfer our main, taxable brokerage account, my two IRAs (one contributory IRA and one rollover IRA from my previous job) and Lynette's two IRAs (one contributory IRA and one SEP-IRA, a type of retirement account for self-employed individuals).

By the time we were done, we had switched over a total of five new accounts, set up a password for Web access, chosen another password for phone access, filled out signature cards, set up "money links" between our local bank and our brokerage, and, finally, arranged for direct deposits between our employers and our bank. As if all that weren't enough, we decided to get brand-new credit cards that would give us frequent-flier mile rewards.

Lynette: All I can say is, this better be worth it.

Lewis: [Gulp] It will all work out, honey. I promise.

And? How Is the Portfolio Performing?

The Model Portfolio finally came to be on March 9, 1998—we launched a real money portfolio. The following chart shows that we are right on track to hit our goal—$1 million by April 1, 2015.

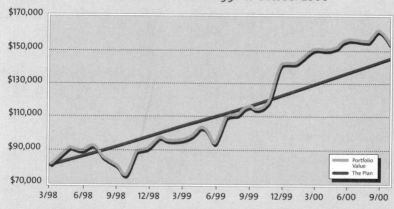

Armchair Millionaire Model Portfolio
Performance March 1998 to October 2000

*How You Can Get Started in the Armchair
Investing Strategy*

The Armchair Investing Strategy is a great way to build your nest egg.
We've selected three mutual funds that represent large U.S. companies, small U.S. companies, and large foreign companies, and invest a
third of our portfolio in each. What's more, the funds we've chosen are
index funds, and each one tracking a particular index that represents
one of the segments of the market listed above.

You can emulate the Armchair Investing Strategy at just about
any brokerage or mutual funds company. You can use it in your own
401(k) account, or in an IRA or Roth IRA, or in a regular taxable
nonretirement account—or all of the above.

How to Choose a Broker: Look at the Funds They Offer

If you'd like to use the Armchair Investing Strategy at a brokerage
firm (either a discount, full-service, or online firm) or at a mutual
fund company, you should look at a few things to help you make
your decision. Since you won't need the advice of a stock broker to
help you implement the Armchair Investing Strategy, you won't
need to pay the high commissions of a full-service broker. A full-
service broker might offer three funds that match the Armchair Millionaire Strategy, but those funds may carry a "load," a commission
that you'll pay when you buy or sell the fund, or both.

The first criterion, of course, is to look for a company that offers
the three funds that we use in the Armchair Investing Strategy:

- Large U.S. Company Index Fund
- Small U.S. Company Index Fund
- Large Foreign Company Index Fund

Once you've found a firm that offers the funds you need, then check
that the firm has reasonable transaction fees for buying and selling

funds. Some brokerage firms charge $25 or more every time you buy a mutual fund. If you were investing $100 a month, a $25 transaction fee would wipe out a big chunk of each monthly investment. Many have no fees at all, at least for most of the funds in their program. These are often called "no-transaction fee" funds, and these are perfect for Armchair Millionaires. Here's a list of firms that are ideal for implementing the Armchair Investing Strategy:

- Charles Schwab
- E*Trade
- Fidelity
- Vanguard
- Waterhouse Securities
- Strong Funds
- T. Rowe Price
- TIAA-CREF

Each of these firms has a variety of index funds available and commission structures that make the Armchair Investing Strategy very inexpensive. (Complete contact information for these firms is available in Appendix C.)

Look for Asset Allocation Funds
ADVICE FROM RICH

Some mutual fund and brokerage companies offer mutual funds that invest in the stock market according to an asset-allocation strategy that is similar to the Armchair Investing Strategy. For instance, the Charles Schwab Market Track Portfolios and the Fidelity Four-in-One Index Fund are alternatives Armchair Millionaires might use instead of buying three separate mutual funds. Generally speaking, these "funds of funds" have slightly higher expenses, but the advantage is that the fund maintains its asset allocation so you can invest in one fund instead of three.

Other Products and Services Offered by Brokerages

There are many other services that brokerage firms may offer that can affect your decision to work with that particular company. Lynette and Lewis outline a number of factors that they considered in selecting their broker:

- Availability of local branch offices. Some investors like knowing that their broker has a nearby office where you can turn if you ever have problems. While online brokers are very convenient, they don't maintain bricks and mortar offices in towns and cities across the country.
- Toll-free telephone support available twenty-four hours a day. Many financial services firms are cutting back on customer support, which could mean limited office hours or that you would have to make a long distance telephone call when you need help.
- Fees and expenses. Many brokers charge hefty fees for opening or closing an account, transferring shares in or out of the account, or maintaining an account that's below a certain minimum balance (often $10,000 or $25,000). Every dollar you pay in fees reduces your overall return, and it doesn't take much for the fees to add up to a sizable chunk of a new investor's portfolio.
- Types of accounts. Most investors need retirement and non-retirement accounts, so make sure your broker offers the types of IRA, Roth IRA, SEP-IRA (if you're self-employed), and other accounts you'll need. One advantage of consolidating your accounts at one brokerage is that the firm may offer additional services or lower fees if the total value of all your accounts is greater than a certain amount, say $100,000. Sticking with one broker can also be more convenient for you when it comes to record-keeping and managing your portfolio.

If You Don't Have a Lot of Money to Invest

Many firms require an initial deposit of $1,000 or more in order to open an account. But if you don't have that much in the bank already, don't panic. Some firms will waive the minimum initial deposit requirement if you sign up for automatic deposits. Here, an Armchair Millionaire describes how he cleared this obstacle.

Getting Started with a Minimum Investment

"T. Rowe Price will allow you to start a mutual fund with no minimum deposit—all you have to do is promise to deposit at least $50 a month via direct deposit. The form they send you to open the account doesn't mention this feature, however. To open the account with no initial deposit, leave the initial deposit section blank, and simply fill out the automatic deposit section, attach your blank check, and you're ready to go. T. Rowe Price has several index funds to choose from. There are probably other mutual fund companies that waive the initial minimum if you agree to automatic deposits. I found out about this from an article on Morningstar.com (the mutual fund rating company)."

—Armchair Millionaire member khuyck

Working with Your Current Brokerage or Fund Company

You may already have an account at a brokerage firm or mutual fund company—does that mean you have to transfer your accounts to a new place? Not at all. While the paperwork required to transfer your portfolio to a new firm isn't particularly complex, it's still *paperwork*—and nobody loves paperwork. In fact, one of the advantages of the Armchair Investing Strategy is that you can do it just about anywhere, including in a company-sponsored retirement account, such as a 401(k).

Emulating the Armchair Investing Strategy

In order to put the Armchair Investing Strategy to work in an existing account, you'll need to find three funds that come closest to the Armchair approach. Check to see if your 401(k) plan, fund company, or broker offers index funds that track the same indexes the Armchair Millionaire uses: the S&P 500, the Russell 2000, and the Morgan Stanley EAFE.

If your plan doesn't offer index funds that are based on those exact same indexes, next check to see if your plan has any index funds that follow a different large company, small company, or international index not used in the Armchair Investing Strategy. For instance, you may be able to find a small-cap stock index fund that tracks the S&P Small Cap 600 instead of the Russell 2000.

ADVICE FROM RICH

If you want to use the Armchair Investing Strategy and your 401(k) plan just doesn't seem to offer the right funds, talk to the people in your company who manage the 401(k) program and see if they will consider adding some more funds to the plan.

Alternatives to Index Funds: Using Active Funds

If your plan comes up short on offering index funds, next turn to actively managed funds. You'll want to look for no-load mutual funds that meet these three criteria:

1. Select funds that invest in the same kinds of companies as the Armchair Investing Strategy suggests. Here's a table of the corresponding categories used by various mutual funds rating and research services to describe the same underlying approaches to the three indexes used in our plan:

Type of Companies	Underlying Index	Category
Large U.S.	S&P 500	Large Growth, Growth & Income, Large Cap
Small U.S.	Russell 2000	Small Cap, Small Blend
Large Foreign	EAFE	Foreign Stock, Non-U.S. Equity

2. Look for funds that have low expense ratios—this is the percentage of the fund that its managers keep to pay for expenses. All other things considered, a fund that has lower expenses should provide a higher rate of return for shareholders.

Here are the average expense ratios for actively managed funds in the three categories used in the Strategy, according to the Investment Company Institute:

Fund Category	Average Expense Ratio
Growth & Income (Large Growth)	1.30%
Small Cap	1.62%
Non-U.S. Equity	1.89%

It's worth noting that the average S&P 500 Index fund has an expense ratio of 0.7 percent, nearly half the cost of an actively managed fund. That's money in your pocket!

3. Look for funds that have a good track record over the past five and ten years. Don't worry about what funds may have been "hot" last year. Look for funds that have performed well over the long term, since you'll be holding your funds for the long term as well.

Putting the Pieces Together
"If you're wondering how all the pieces of your portfolio fit together, think of them as a whole unit, rather than separate com-

ponents. For instance, my 401(k) is invested in an S&P 500 fund, so I have all my 401(k) money going into that. I have my IRA and Keogh money in small caps (Russell 2000). I currently have my taxable investments in the S&P 500, but am in the process of switching it to an EAFE Index. Look at your portfolio as a whole, not in pieces."

—Armchair Millionaire member am_bo

Now that you know how the Armchair Investing Strategy works, you need to know how much money to invest in each of the three stock index funds that make up the portfolio. This is the simplest part of the Armchair Investing Strategy—you just invest an equal portion in each. For every $1,000 that you invest in the Armchair Investing Strategy, you should put $333.33 into each index fund. For many people, the decision to invest in the stock market is fraught with anxiety. The Armchair Investing Strategy is so simple to use— and so effective—that it helps take the worry out of managing a portfolio. It doesn't matter what long-term goals you might be striving to reach, whether it's a comfortable retirement, college education for your kids, a forty-foot sailboat, or a summer home in the mountains—the Armchair Investing Strategy is your key to becoming a millionaire.

Composing Your Portfolio by Time Horizon

The Armchair Investing Strategy is a long-term approach to the stock market. You should only use it for money that you're willing to set aside for at least five years. If you have short-term goals, such as paying for college tuition for your kids, or a first home, or a big wedding, then you should implement a modified version of the Armchair Investing Strategy.

First, examine your time frame—how long until you will need your funds? For every year fewer than five, put 15 percent of your investments into a more conservative investment, such as a bond index fund, or a money market fund. That way, that percentage of your money won't be hurt if the stock market takes a hit. So if you are going to need your money in a year, make sure 60 percent (15% x 4 years) of your money is out of the stock market.

If you're sixty-five and already retired, you're probably looking forward to ten or more years of golden living, so you should still set aside part of your portfolio in a five- or ten-year plan like the Armchair Investing Strategy.

Chapter 8 Action Items

- Find a brokerage firm that you like, that has low fees, and that offers index funds in different sub-asset classes.
- Set up an automatic investment plan.
- Invest one-third of your long-term portfolio in stock market mutual funds that track these (or equivalent) indexes:

> Standard & Poor's 500
> Russell 2000
> Morgan Stanley EAFE

- If your financial institution doesn't offer index funds that match the Armchair Millionaire approach, you should invest in three actively managed funds that match the Armchair Investing Strategy.
- Breathe easy, knowing that your investment plan is running on autopilot.

STEP 5:
Start Today—Put the Power of Compound Interest to Work for You

By now, we hope you've learned the importance of saving your money and investing it regularly in the stock market. You've also learned why it's so important to "Pay Yourself First," and to take advantage of tax-deferred retirement plans like 401(k) accounts and IRAs. What could possibly be left to know about investing, you may wonder?

Well, there is one more step, one last action that you have to undertake before you can reach your million-dollar goal. In fact, we've saved the single most important step of the Armchair Millionaire plan for last. This is the true secret to building wealth, and perhaps the most important bit of financial advice that you may ever receive.

What is the key to financial freedom? It's this:

START TODAY.

Sounds like a no-brainer, right? But actually, there's a formidable stack of academic research, mathematical calculations, and supercharged thinking that have gone into the development of this key piece of the Armchair Investing Strategy. All of this knowledge has been crystallized into these two words, the two most important words you should remember even if you forget everything else we've told you in this book (though we certainly hope you'll remember a bit more).

The Power of Compound Interest

How can an uncomplicated command like this be so critical to the building of a million-dollar portfolio? It comes down to the power of time. You should put your money to work in a sensible investing plan so that eventually you won't have to work. Time is money, as the saying goes, but the opposite is also true—money is time. The sooner you put your money to work for you, the greater it will grow. This is because of the miracle of *compound interest.*

One of the greatest minds of the twentieth century, Albert Einstein, pondered the many secrets of the universe (including that famous formula about relativity that every school kid can recite). But even Einstein was supposedly astounded at how compound interest worked. Legend has it he called it "the eighth wonder of the world." (There's been some question about whether Einstein ever said any such thing, but it's such a good story that we had to include it here.)

What's so amazing about compound interest? Compound interest is simply what happens when you put some money in a bank account that earns interest. After the bank makes the first interest payment in the account, that interest begins to earn interest. Sure, at first your interest seems pretty puny, but over time, all that interest earning interest causes your account to grow at a higher rate.

Suppose you invest $1.00 and leave it alone for ten years at 10 percent interest. After a year, your dollar would be worth $1.10. In the second year, that 10 percent interest would be calculated on $1.10, not $1.00, so you'll have $1.21 after the second year, After a decade, you would have $2.59—more than double your original investment—and with no additional savings put in. The effects of compounding simply grow stronger over time. After two hundred years, your original dollar would be worth $190 million!

In an investment account, the same thing happens, only we call it "compound returns." Your investments will grow and earn interest, dividends, and capital gains. And then those returns start to earn returns, etc., etc. Sure, it sounds simple, but over the course of time, the effects are nothing short of awesome.

Here's a quiz that might help you understand the amazing powers of compounding.

You are offered a temporary job for thirty days. You have to choose between two different payment plans:

1) $1,000 a day for thirty days, *or*
2) A penny for the first day, two cents the next day, four cents for the third day, and your pay would double like that every day for thirty days.

Which do you choose? If you chose the first payment method, that's too bad. The good news is you'll make $30,000 for 30 days' work (nice work if you can get it!).

Here's the bad news: If you chose the second payment plan, you're going to take home over $10 million ($10,737,418.23, to be exact) instead of the $30,000 that you would have made with choice #1. That's the power of compounding at work!

Check out the math.

Payment plan 1
$1,000 a day for 30 days
$1,000 × 30 days = $30,000

Payment plan 2
A penny for the first day, two cents the next day, four cents for the third day, and your pay would double like that every day for thirty days. Here's how it would look:

Day	Payment	Cumulative Total
1	.01	.01
2	.02	.03
3	.04	.07
4	.08	.15
5	.16	.31
6	.32	.63
7	.64	1.27
8	1.28	2.55
9	2.56	5.11
10	5.12	10.23
11	10.24	20.47
12	20.48	40.95
13	40.96	81.91
14	81.92	163.83
15	163.84	327.67
16	327.68	655.35
17	655.36	1,310.71
18	1310.72	2,621.43
19	2,621.44	5,242.87
20	5,242.88	10,485.75
21	10,585.76	20,971.51
22	20,971.52	41,943.03
23	41,943.04	83,886.07
24	83,886.08	167,772.15
25	167,772.16	335,544.31
26	335,544.32	671,088.63
27	671,088.64	1,342,177.27
28	1,342,177.28	2,684,354.55
29	2,684,354.56	5,368,709.11
30	5,368,709.12	10,737,418.23

TOTAL: $10,737,418.23

Now, do you still think that it's not worth it to invest a small amount of money? We didn't think so.

A *Tale of Two Teenagers*

Nicole is a smart kid. Her parents have explained compound interest to her, and so she knows how to invest a gift of $2,000 that she receives on her eighteenth birthday. Nicole puts the entire amount in an Armchair Millionaire portfolio of mutual funds that returns 10 percent each year.

Then she keeps investing $2,000 each year for three more years. Then she stops to join a rock and roll band. Nicole's total investment: $8,000. At age sixty-five, Nicole will have $615,063 from her original investment of $8,000. *Nicole's parents love her.* Especially after she quit the band and went back to college.

Charlie wasn't loved as a child . . . Charlie's parents didn't teach him the value of compound interest. He doesn't start investing until he's thirty. But when Charlie does finally start investing, he invests $2,000 each year. Just like Nicole.

Charlie keeps investing $2,000 *for the next thirty-five years.* Unfortunately, even if Charlie keeps putting away $2,000 every year, for the next thirty-five years—**for a total of $70,000 invested**—he'll still have *less* than Nicole.

After thirty-five years, Charlie will have $596,254. Almost $20,000 less than Nicole, even though he invested nearly eight times as much as she did. Time really is money.

The Lesson: Understand the power of compounding interest. Worship it. Show it how much you love it by starting your investing plan today. Oh, and be nice to your kids.

Compound Interest in Action

Okay, okay, so compounding interest is great. But what if you're well past your early adulthood? Of course, you can't turn back the clock—so if you didn't start investing at an early age, there's nothing you can do about it now. But you can decide to not let any more time go by before you begin your financial plan. That's why "Start Today" is so beautiful—you can heed its advice at any age. To help you take the plunge, listen to these real life Armchair Millionaires.

A Real Life Someone Who Started Early . . .

"I started saving money at the age of sixteen. At twenty-three, I bought my first house with a cash deposit of 25 percent (about everything I had in the bank account). Now, I'm thirty and have almost paid for my house. At the bank, I have the same amount of money I earn in a year. At forty-five, if everything goes right, I'll have enough money to retire. The only thing I would not do if I had to do it all again, I wouldn't have paid for my house that fast, so that the money I put into the house could have grown more."

—Armchair Millionaire member Let it grow!

Versus a Real Life Someone Who Didn't

"I enjoyed my twenties, but I wish I had saved more instead of spending money on clothes, cars, bar-hopping, and such. I lived rent-free until I was twenty-six. Had I plunked even $250 a month into an investment vehicle, I would have a substantially larger sum of money tucked away than I do now. I started to invest at age twenty-eight, and currently at age thirty-two have a portfolio worth $44,000. I kick myself thinking about what I could have if I had gotten smart a few years earlier. I now have a well paying job but I also have a wife, child, and mortgage. It's harder to find the money to save now than it would have been ten years ago."

—Armchair Millionaire member Michael

A Ray of Hope

"I think a lot of us buy into the fairy tale that things will work out all right in the end. We grew up in a mad advertising world of 'buy now, cry later.' So we are all paying for it with no freedom, as many of us—regardless of income—struggle to make it to the next paycheck.

> But now that we know how to save and invest, we can do something about it. Even if it is a minimal amount at first, we must all begin somewhere. I started with $20 per paycheck and proceeded to pay off all my debts. I am down to one loan that will be paid off in a few months, and I am planning on buying a condo next spring. Not bad for someone who could not afford the rent three years ago."
>
> —Armchair Millionaire member Raymond D.

From the Armchair Millionaire's Gallery

How Compound Interest Has the Power to Turn You into an "Accidental Millionaire," with Special Guest Star, Professor Andrew Hacker

There is more to making compounding interest work for you than simply starting now. The second half of the final step in the Armchair Millionaire plan is to leave the money that you have invested where it is. Because if you dip into those funds, you'll not only reduce your immediate returns, but over time your compounded returns will suffer. However, if you leave those funds whole, you can harness the true power of compound interest. Take for example the story of Professor Andrew Hacker. The author of *Money: Who Has How Much and Why* started his career as a humble college instructor who never imagined that he had the astuteness needed to make money in the market (if only he had had the Armchair Millionaire program to follow!). All he did in regard to investing was to steadily deduct a percentage of his paycheck and put it into his university retirement account at Teachers Insurance and Annuity Association-College Retirement Equities Fund, known as TIAA-CREF (TIAA-CREF is a leading provider of retirement plans for educational institutions). He didn't even look at his balance until it came time for him to retire. What he found when he finally did look is nothing short of astounding.

Name: Professor Andrew Hacker

Age: Late 60s

Occupation: I'm a college professor. I'm officially retired, but I'm still teaching a full load of classes because I like to.

How long have you been investing?

Well, I've never officially invested on my own—all I have done is had a certain percentage deducted from my paycheck into my pension fund. I started that over forty years ago, when I started teaching.

Was it difficult for you to give up that portion of your paycheck?

My first salary as an instructor was $4,500 a year. And my deduction into my pension was 7.5 percent, and the university matched another 7.5 percent. Even though I wasn't making that much money, not having that 7.5 percent felt just ordinary, like any other payroll deduction.

When you started out what were your financial goals?

As a college professor, I knew I wasn't going to get rich. Until I went to my first job at Cornell and I was taken under the wing of a professor who did outside writing. With his help, I discovered that you can be a college professor, which is a nice, worthy occupation, and still become quite comfortable. The goal was always not wealth but comfort.

How far along are you now?

I've reached my goal. That is to say, more comes in than I need.

How did you realize that your financial goals had been met?

Now I am a professor at the City University of New York, and a few years ago I was eligible for retirement. At the time, they were having a budget crunch. And of course, when they cut positions, they cut from the bottom, even when it might make more sense to take aim at full professors sitting on fat salaries. I'm not Saint Andrew, but I realized I was getting a salary that was the equivalent of three junior people's. So I called up my fund administrators, and found out that the total in my retirement account was $1.1 million dollars. I was flabbergasted! This shows you the value of compound interest—not just the investments—but forty years of compound interest. Wow.

How did your life change after you realized that your years of investing had paid off?
My generation, I call it the Eisenhower generation, we got on an escalator and we just moved up. I'm a pretty good guy, but I didn't deserve everything I got. It was just a historical happenstance. So I set up a trust fund for my daughter and her husband because I felt I should share.

And there's only been one other real change: I now fly to Europe in business class. And I have flown the Concorde once. It was fun. There were about sixty other people on it. And I realized that all these people were regulars—they knew the stewardesses, they were busy working on their laptops. We landed at Kennedy airport at 9 A.M., and there was no one else there because no other flights had arrived yet. And there were fifty-nine limousines lined up to pick the regular Concorde passengers up! My wife and I were the only ones who took a cab.

What advice would you give someone who wants to begin investing?
Speaking as an outsider, if I were to invest, I hope I would be prudent enough to put it all into an index fund. I'm smart, but in no way am I smart enough to beat the market. I know some people do, but there isn't that much smartness around. And my second piece of gratuitous advice is to get married and stay married. Two can live as cheaply as 1.7, so you will have extra money. And if you don't get divorced, you don't have child support, you don't have a second household to keep up, all those things. I was married for more than forty years, and it was important.

Put Compounding to Work Today

The secret ingredient of compounding isn't skill, nor is it luck or knowledge. It's nothing more than time. By starting now, you can put its mighty force to work.

But, there's a catch (there's always a catch). The longer you procrastinate on your investment plan, the less effective the law of compounding becomes. If you don't believe it, turn back to page 165 and see what your total pay would have been if you had only worked twenty-five days. Those first five days didn't seem that important (after all, you only brought home 31 cents). But without them, you'd only have $335,544.31 after twenty-five days instead of the whopping $10,737,418.23 you'd accrue after thirty. That's why you need time on your side—and why you must *start today*.

When you put money into an investment, you earn returns in the form of interest, dividends and capital gains. The value of your investment compounds when these returns themselves start to earn returns. *Over time, this compounding will be the most important ingredient to building your fortune.*

ADVICE FROM RICH

When calculating the returns of your portfolio, you may have gains from any or all of three sources. *Interest* is the money you earn on cash that's held in a bank or money market account. *Dividends* are a share of the profits that a company may pay its stockholders, usually four times a year. *Capital gains* are the profits from stocks or other securities that have appreciated (increased) in price since you first purchased those shares. If you own a stock or security that has increased in price, you are said to be holding "unrealized capital gains"; you "realize" the gains when you sell the shares (and in the process create a tax liability, since realized capital gains are subject to taxes.)

When you add up all three of these, dividends, interest, capital gains (realized and/or unrealized), you can determine the **total return** of an investment.

The secret ingredient to compounding is no more than time—so the sooner you start your investment plan, the longer you have for compounding to work its powerful magic. *Start today!*

> ### ADVICE FROM RICH
>
> Here's a nifty trick for figuring out the impact of compounding on your investments, known as the Rule of 72. Here's how it works: Divide 72 by your expected annual rate of return. The result is the number of years until your investment doubles. So, suppose you expect to get an average yearly return of 10 percent. 72 divided by 10 equals 7.2. Your investment would double in just over seven years. How's that for an enjoyable math problem?

Putting It All Together

So let's take a look at just exactly how the Five Steps work together to help you to reach your million-dollar goal.

Consider Fred, the prototypical Armchair Millionaire. He's thirty years old, and earns a salary of about $45,000 a year, taking home about $3,000 a month after taxes.

Fred has been saving a bit here and there, and has saved up about $10,000 in the bank. He also knows enough to be investing in his 401(k) at work, and is now contributing $300 each month to the plan. Over the past few years, his 401(k) has grown to be about $10,000.

In order to become a millionaire, here's what Fred needs to do:

Step #1. Fred needs to max out his 401(k) plan each month. He should increase his monthly contribution to $562, which is 15 percent of his pretax monthly salary. This will allow him to contribute $6,750 a year to his 401(k) plan. If he gets a pay raise of 3 percent a year, he should increase his 401(k) contribution accordingly. In twenty-one years, Fred will have contributed a total of $203,394 to his plan.

Step #2. Fred needs to pay himself first. Each month, before paying any other bills, Fred should set aside 10 percent of his after-tax income for his Armchair Millionaire plan, which comes out to $300 a month. Assuming his salary increases on average about 3 percent a year, he should increase his "Pay Yourself First" contribution by the same amount—more if he can afford it. And if he signs up for a money-link program with a bank or brokerage, that money will be automatically withdrawn from his account each month, saving the hassle of remembering to write a check. In twenty-one years, these savings will come to a total of $113,235.

At this point, Fred will have saved a total of $316,629. While that's not chicken feed, it's far short of a million dollars. But that's okay, as you'll see once we invest that money for Fred.

Step #3. Fred should invest each month, both in his 401(k) account and in a taxable account at a brokerage firm or mutual fund company (using his "Pay Yourself First" money). He shouldn't let the money sit around, or try to "time" the market. He needs to invest each and every month, regardless of how high or low the market may be. His broker or mutual fund can handle this, automating the process.

Step #4. Fred should invest according to the Armchair Millionaire Investing Strategy, dividing up his investments into three pieces. He will invest a third into a U.S. large-cap stock index fund (like an S&P 500 index fund); a third into a U.S. small-cap stock index fund (one that imitates the Russell 2000, for instance); and one-third into a foreign large-cap stock index fund (one that tracks the EAFE index). This will provide him with the proper diversification and optimum return at the least risk.

Step #5. Fred should let his portfolio ride. He should continually add more money to his accounts and let the returns compound continuously.

If Fred can manage these five steps, and if his portfolios are able to grow just 10 percent a year on average, the value of his investments will be a million dollars in twenty-one years. Fred didn't need to win the lottery, or be a genius investor. Investing sensibly, the Armchair Millionaire way, is all it takes.

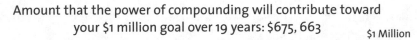

Amount that the power of compounding will contribute toward your $1 million goal over 19 years: $675, 663

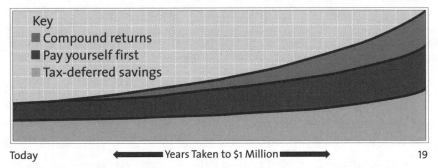

- Fred's current tax-deferred savings: $10,000
- Fred's ongoing investments: $800 each month; amount in Fred's tax-deferred investment accounts in nineteen years: $251,122
- Amount Fred pays himself each month: $300 (10 percent of his take-home pay); total saved in nineteen years: $100,421.
- Amount that the power of compounding will contribute towards Fred's $1 million goal over nineteen years: $675,663.
  GRAND TOTAL: $1,000,000

This is what the power of compounding will do for your investments on the way to your million-dollar goal. Time is the secret ingredient for accomplishing your goal. So start now, already!

Chapter 9 Action Items

In this chapter, you've learned how compound returns are the secret of a million dollar portfolio.

It's imperative that you start your plan today. Follow the steps in this book, and you can join the ranks of Armchair Millionaires from all around the world.

CHAPTER 10

Fulfilling Your Dreams

Now you've read all about the five steps that can help you to achieve all your long-term financial goals and provide you with the confidence that you'll need to build real wealth. Up until this point, we've talked about all the work you'll have to do in order to achieve your financial dreams. Of course, according to the Armchair Millionaire plan, all this striving won't really *feel* like work. But while you're on your way, it's important to remember that as you get older and your portfolio grows, your time frame shrinks. Someday, you will arrive at the target you've been aiming at for many years. How will you know when you've gotten there? What will that be like? And what will you know then that you don't know now?

Before we fast-forward and start answering these questions, there's just one thing left to do. In order to imagine your dreams fulfilled, you first have to know exactly what those dreams are. After all, if you don't know what you want, you're never going to get it. Take some time to daydream about how you want your life to be after you've accumulated enough wealth to live comfortably. Do you want to travel the country in a Winnebago? Or start the business you've always dreamed about? Whatever it is, get a good image in your mind of what you look like doing it. This picture will help carry you through any rough times you might experience along the way.

While Visions of Armchair Millionaires Danced in Their Heads

Are you curious to see how your financial goals compare to others'? Here members of the Armchair Millionaire community talk frankly about where they want to be in twenty years.

Looking at the (Very) Long Term

"I'm going to retire from my job as a firefighter in eight years (at age fifty-six) with a good pension. Once I retire I plan to work at jobs that I enjoy, such as a flight instructor, a helicopter pilot for tour operators in exotic locations, or a river guide. I also plan on living to one hundred! So I don't plan on withdrawing money from my tax-deferred accounts until I'm seventy and a half. By that time I should have a very big nest egg that should allow me and my wife to live a most comfortable final thirty years."

—Armchair Millionaire member Knucklehead

Aiming to Live Stress-Free

"I would like the ability to retire by the age of forty-five but would love to continue working until sixty. Providing for my son and traveling are my highest goals. Freedom from stress is all I need."

—Armchair Millionaire member Isaac

A Call to Action

"My long-term goal is to be in a financial position to be able to enjoy life to its fullest, and be free from the job that controls my life as I trade hours for dollars. My short-term goals are to reach financial independence working for myself, and showing others how to do the same. It's a wondrous world out there. Let's get out from behind those desks, choose the hours that we want to work (or not work), spend our time making ourselves wealthy (instead of our companies), and see this world at our leisure (instead of on the week-long "vacations" our bosses allow us to take)!"

—Armchair Millionaire member Cindy

FAST-FORWARD

Let's pretend that it is twenty years from now. You've been following your Armchair Millionaire plan for financial freedom. How will you know when you start to reach the goals you've been striving for for so long? Of course, it depends on how you define those goals— either your portfolio will reach a designated number, or the income from your investments will be such that you can stop working for a living. Maybe you'll finally be able to fund a new business enterprise without jeopardizing your standard of living. Or you'll be able to quit your job and dedicate your time to a charitable cause. There are many ways to see your dreams coming true.

In very basic terms, you'll know you've reached your destination when you don't have to worry about money anymore. This doesn't mean that you'll have a lavish, indulgent lifestyle. In true Armchair Millionaire fashion, you'll have a peace of mind that comes from being satisfied with what you have, and with having more than you need.

A Day in the Life of a Millionaire

Let's take a closer look at the future and see what it's really like to live your life as a millionaire.

The first thing you'll do every morning is wake up in a house that you have already paid for. This house will most likely be in a very nice, but not flashy, neighborhood. The house itself will have more room than you absolutely need without being a sprawling testament to the size of your bank account.

Over breakfast, you can read the paper for ideas on where to take your next vacation. You may look for news about your investments, or you may skip the financial section altogether, knowing that your portfolio is still functioning on autopilot. Perhaps your daughter will call from college—where she is enjoying a paid-for education (and if she's the offspring of an Armchair Millionaire, chances are she's working a little on the side to help minimize her living expenses and to get a head start on her own portfolio.)

After breakfast, you'll climb into your reliable, debt-free car and drive to the job you've taken because it's so much fun you'd do the work for free. Perhaps it's a new business that was spawned out of a hobby, or a part-of-the-year job that also gives you the flexibility to travel. Or maybe you'll take up painting, and furnish all your relatives' homes with original works of art.

You'll be able to do all this without any worry, because your finances are completely in order. You said good-bye to credit card debt long ago. You're well insured to protect against emergencies. And you have a will set up to insure that your hard work will continue to pay off even after you're gone. And of course, your investment portfolio is still growing, generating interest and a favorable rate of return.

It sounds pretty nice, doesn't it?

More Than Just Money

While you're thinking about your goals, keep in mind your ideals. Here, an Armchair Millionaire who is also an actual millionaire talks about how money is not all there is.

Think Outside the Box

"I am thirty-seven and made it into the millionaire club last year, but now I realize that money alone cannot give you happiness, you need more in life. That certain extra something will differ from person to person. It may take some time and a lot of conviction to achieve it, but the name of the game is to know what you want and then go for it."

—Posted by FAIZAN

From the Armchair Millionaire's Gallery—
Looks Like He's Made It

Armchair Millionaire Member Name: CanQuitAnytime

From: Gainesville, Florida

Age: 48

Occupation: Construction Manager

Family Status: Married

Financial goals: Complete financial independence with a middle-class lifestyle. My secondary goal is to use my estate to help future generations of my family.

How far along are you?

Actually, I am there but every day I work improves the quality of my lifestyle when I do retire. Also, there will be that much more for my kids.

How long have you been investing?

Since May 1980

What got you started?

The year after I got married, I had to pay taxes on two incomes. The tax bite was horrible and it took both my wife's and my paychecks and what little savings we had. Ever since, I have been budgeting, saving, and investing.

What was your biggest misconception before you started investing?

I thought that investing was for rich people. I thought little guys like me just had savings accounts.

What was the biggest investment mistake you ever made?

I got into day trading and options. I confused an 'up market' with investing savvy. I programmed my computer to analyze all types of stock and option combinations, covered calls, spreads, and so on. When the market turned down, I lost *big time*. It set me back over a year.

What did you learn from that mistake?
The only real way to create wealth is to make a business plan for yourself. Know what your expenses are. Not just from month to month, but for the next five, ten, and twenty years. This includes the next car you will need when the old one finally dies, college and weddings for kids, and so on. Understand how much you have to sell in order to realize the extra income you need to pay for all these expenses and still save for investments.

What milestones do you most remember about your financial journey?
I remember the first time I realized the plan was working and I could look forward to early retirement. I can't explain the change it made in my mental disposition. My outlook was altered forever. I also remember when it dawned on me that my estate could be a wonderful legacy for my family. With the right planning, my kids' kids' kids one hundred years from now will go to college and have advantages that others will not, based on investments I am making now.

How is your life different now that you are so much nearer to your financial goals?
I like to say I am married to my wife, not my job. Most of my friends can't say that. When I was in the military, very early on in my career, everyone wanted to just make it twenty years and then retire. I swore that [kind of obligation to a job] would never happen to me. And guess what! By saving and investing, it never did.

What advice would you give to someone who is just beginning to plan for attaining her financial goals?
1. Get control of your cash flow (track every penny).

2. If you are not saving at least 10 percent of your salary as well as maxing out your retirement plans, you are living above your means.

3. Understand what you invest in (educate yourself) and invest for the long term.

4. Money and work isn't everything. If you aren't having fun, you are in the wrong job.

Listening to Your Future Self

Now that you can see what life will be like as a millionaire, can you imagine what kind of advice the millionaire-you would give the now-you? It might go something like this:

"I know it seems like a long road to get to where you don't have to worry about money. But the sooner you start, the easier it will be, and the sooner you can start to enjoy it. Trust me, the things you have to give up to invest are definitely worth the security you'll have later in life. What's a fancy new piece of stereo equipment or pretty new dress compared to a worry-free retirement? That dress will be out of style in less than a year, and the stereo equipment will be obsolete in two. Get your plan set up today and it will work for you for years to come. I can tell you that you are really going to love financial freedom. Sorry I can't talk more, but I'm late for my tee time!"

This might seem like a silly exercise, but a little forethought will only make your plan stronger.

What I Wish I Had Known— Armchair Millionaires Share Their Tips

Luckily, you don't have to rely solely on your imagination to get advice from those who have already achieved their financial goals. Below, Armchair Millionaires share the wisdom they know now and wish they had known then.

Do Your Research

"The one thing I wish I knew when I started investing was to read, read, read. Books, magazines, and newspapers give you the full picture—the kind of info you'll never get all on your own."

—Armchair Millionaire member Pamela

Investigate Your Sources

"You have to be very aware of whom you take advice from when it comes to money. Most people have agendas when it comes to financial advice—brokers are especially guilty of this."

—Armchair Millionaire member Inanka

'Nuff Said

"I wish I'd never listened to my brother-in-law."

—Armchair Millionaire member Clain

Talk to Other Like-Minded Investors

"I wish I had been on the message boards of sites like Armchair Millionaire before I started investing. When you get a lot of different opinions, you learn how to form your own."

—Armchair Millionaire member Ash

Stop Looking for the Pot of Gold

"I wish I had known to invest for the long term in well-known blue chips versus trying to hit the home run with penny stocks and losing all my money year after year."

—Armchair Millionaire member Sharon

Don't Wait

"I wish I'd understood how even a small amount saved and invested each month would grow into a substantial amount over time. I would have started sooner."

—Armchair Millionaire member Katie

Action Items for Chapter 10

- Get a good image of your future self enjoying the benefits of years' worth of investing. What will you be doing? And what advice will you be giving to folks about investing?
- Get started on your investment plan today. Dreams will still only be dreams if you don't start now.

Appendices

How to Use the Armchair Millionaire Web Site and This Book

This book was born on the Internet! It's a companion to Armchair-Millionaire.com (http://www.armchairmillionaire.com), a Web site that was founded in 1997 in order to help ordinary people learn commonsense strategies for saving and investing. Every month, thousands and thousands of people visit ArmchairMillionaire.com looking for advice and information. Like you, they're all trying to find their way toward a better financial future.

Together, they make up a community of people just like you— people who want to become financially independent without budgeting all the fun out of their lives.

When you visit Armchair Millionaire on the Web, you'll find plenty of information that we just couldn't fit into this book. Here's a taste of what you'll find there . . .

The Five Steps to Financial Freedom
Learn even more about the five simple steps that can make you a millionaire. We've even got a cool interactive tool that will help you create your own customized plan for saving and investing. Enter a few details, and we'll explain it all, step by step, and give you an action plan at the end that you can use to get started. Thousands of people in the Armchair Millionaire community have already put these time-tested principles to work, and you'll meet some of them

here. You'll also find the essential tools and information you'll need to get started on your own path to financial freedom.

The Model Portfolio

Countdown with Lewis and Lynette as they invest their real money and turn it into a million-dollar portfolio using the Five Steps to Financial Freedom. You'll get current updates and tips as their portfolio grows and grows.

Armchair Millionaire Communities

We've created several areas on our site, each devoted to a different topic. We call them our "communities," and it's here that you'll find more specific answers to questions on many of the concepts we've covered in this book. Here are the three main communities:

GETTING STARTED

The name says it all. Paying off debt? Just beginning to set aside a few bucks? Jump in and get started!

SAVVY INVESTING

Here you'll learn all about the options that will help you save and invest in the stock market.

FUND-AMENTALS

You'll find all you need to know about mutual funds, from the basics of fund investing to advanced asset allocation strategies.

Finally, be sure to check out **The Armchair Millionaire's Gallery.** Here you can meet real people on their way to financial freedom— and a few who have already arrived.

Index Funds You Can Use in the Armchair Investing Strategy

Standard & Poor's 500 Index Funds

The first component of the Armchair Investing Strategy is to invest in U.S. large cap stocks, preferably in an S&P 500 index fund.

Fund Information	Initial Investment	
	Regular	IRA
Advantus Index 500 Fund A (ADIAX) 800-665-6005 http://www.advantusfunds.com	$250	$250
Aetna Index Plus Large Cap A (AELAX) 800-367-7732 http://www.aeltus.com/aetnafunds	$1,000	$500
Aon S&P 500 Index (ASPYX) http://www.aon.com	$1,000	—
Bankers Trust Pyramid Equity 500 Index (BTIEX) Bankers Trust and its affiliated companies have been acquired by Deutsche Bank	$2,500	$500
California Investment Trust S&P 500 Index (SPFIX) 800-225-8778 http://www.caltrust.com	$5,000	$5,000
Dreyfus S&P 500 Index (PEOPX) 800-221-1793 http://www.dreyfus.com	$2,500	$750

Fund Information	Initial Investment	
	Regular	**IRA**
E*Trade S&P 500 Index (ETSPX) 800-786-2575 http://www.etrade.com	$1,000	$250
Evergreen Select Equity Index A (ESINX) 800-225-2618 http://www.evergreen-funds.com	$1,000	$1,000
Fidelity Spartan Market Index (FSMKX) 800-544-6666 http://personal300.fidelity.com/products/funds	$10,000	$500
First American-Equity Index A (FAEIX) 800-637-2548	$1,000	$250
Galaxy II Large Co. Index (ILCIX) 877-289-4252 http://www.galaxyfunds.com	$2,500	$500
Harris Insight Trust Index (HIDAX) 800-982-8782 http://www.harrisinsight.com	$1,000	$250
Invesco S&P 500 Index (ISPIX) 800-675-1705 http://www.invesco.com	$5,000	$2,000
Kent Index Equity (KNIDX) 800-633-KENT http://www.kentfunds.com	$1,000	$100
MainStay Equity Index A (MCSEX) 800-624-6782 http://www.mainstayfunds.com	$1,000	$1,000
Munder Index 500 A (MUXAX) 800-438-5789 http://www.munder.com	$500	$250
Northern Stock Index (NOSIX) 800-595-9111 http://www.ntrs.com	$2,500	$500
One Group-Equity Index A (OGEAX) 800-338-4345 http://www.onegroup.com	$1,000	$250

Fund Information	Initial Investment	
	Regular	IRA
PIMCO Stocks PLUS Fund A (PSPAX) 800-227-7337 http://www.pimcofunds.com	$2,500	$1,000
Schwab S&P 500 Index (SWPIX) 800-435-4000 http://www.schwab.com	$1,000	$500
Scudder S&P 500 Index (SCPIX) 800-225-2470 http://www.scudder.com	$2,500	$1,000
State Street Global Advisors S&P 500 Index (SVSPX) 800-647-7327 http://www.ssgafunds.com	$10,000	$250
Strong Index 500 (SINEX) 800-359-3379 http://www.strong-funds.com	$2,500	$1,000
Transamerica Premier Index (TPIIX) 800-892-7587 http://www.transamerica.com	$1,000	$250
T. Rowe Price Equity Index (PREIX) 800-225-5132 http://www.troweprice.com/mutual/index.html	$2,500	$1,000
USAA S&P 500 Index (USSPX) 800-382-8722 http://www.usaaedfoundation.org	$3,000	$2,000
Vanguard Index Trust 500 (VFINX) 800-860-8394 http://www.vanguard.com	$3,000	$1,000
Wachovia Equity Index A (BTEIX) 800-994-4414 http://www.wachovia.com	$250	$250
Wells Fargo Equity Index A (SFCSX) 800-552-9612	$1,000	$250

You could also purchase S&P Depository Receipts, known as SPDRs or Spiders. These are exchange-traded funds that own the same stocks in the S&P 500 as an index fund, and have very low expenses. SPDRs trade on the American Stock Exchange under the ticker symbol SPY, and you can purchase them at any brokerage firm.

Small-Cap Stock Index Funds

The second component of the Armchair Investing Strategy is to invest in a small-cap index fund, one that tracks the Russell 2000 (or other small-cap) index as a benchmark.

Fund Information	Initial Investment	
	Regular	IRA
AXP Small Company Index A (ISIAX) 800-328-8300 http://www.americanexpress.com/advisors	$2,000	$50
Federated Mini-Cap C (MNCCX) 800-341-7400 http://www.federatedinvestors.com	$1,500	$250
Galaxy II Small Company Index (ISCIX) 800-628-0414 http://www.galaxyfunds.com	$2,500	$500
Gateway Small Cap Index (GSCIX) 800-354-6339	$1,000	$500
Merrill Lynch Small Cap Index D (MDSKX) 609-282-2800 http://www.ml.com	$1,000	$100
Schwab Small Cap Index (SWSMX) 800-435-4000 http://www.schwab.com	$2,500	$1,000
Vanguard Index Trust Small Cap (NAESX) 800-871-3879 http://www.vanguard.com	$3,000	$1,000

Morgan Stanley EAFE Index Fund

The third piece of the Armchair Investing Strategy is to invest in a global mutual fund, one that uses the MSCI EAFE as its benchmark. MSCI EAFE stands for "Morgan Stanley Capital International—Europe, Australasia, and the Far East," and it tracks stocks in those countries. It's a bit harder to find an index fund that follows the EAFE, so you may have to use an actively managed fund with low expenses instead of an index fund.

Fund Information	Initial Investment	
	Regular	IRA
Dreyfus International Stock Index (DIISX) 800-645-6561 http://www.dreyfus.com	$2,500	$750
E*Trade International Index (ETINX) 800-786-2575 http://www.etrade.com	$1,000	$250
First American International Index A (FIIAX) First American International Index B (FIXBX) 800-637-2548	$1,000	$250
Merrill Lynch International Index D (MDIIX) 800-456-4587 http://www.ml.com	$1,000	$100
One Group Intl Equity Index A (OEIAX) One Group Intl Equity Index B (OGEBX) One Group Intl Equity Index C (OIICX) 800-480-4111 http://www.onegroup.com	$1,000	$250
Schwab International Index (SWINX) 800-435-4000 http://www.schwab.com	$2,500	$1,000
Vanguard Total Intl Stock Index (VGTSX) 800-662-7447 http://www.vanguard.com	$3,000	$1,000

Brokerage Firms and
Mutual Fund Companies

Here are some of the top brokerage firms and mutual fund companies. Call or visit them on the Web to get information on opening an account.

Charles Schwab
800-225-8570
http://www.schwab.com

E*Trade
800-ETRADE-1
http://www.etrade.com

Fidelity
800-544-6666
http://www.fidelity.com

Strong Funds
800-359-3379
http://www.estrong.com

TD Waterhouse
800-934-4448
http://www.tdwaterhouse.com

TIAA-CREF
800 842-2776
http://www.tiaa-cref.org

T. Rowe Price
800-225-5132
http://www.troweprice.com

Vanguard
800-871-3879
http://www.vanguard.com

401(k) Plan: A tax-deferred defined contribution retirement plan offered by an employer.

403(b) Plan: Similar to a 401(k) plan, but offered by nonprofit and educational organizations.

457 Plan: A savings and retirement plan for local and state government employees.

Adjusted Gross Income: The amount of your annual income that the IRS uses to determine the taxes you owe. Certain deductions, known as "adjustments," are subtracted from your total income to determine your AGI. Your AGI is calculated prior to taking itemized or standard deductions.

Armchair Millionaire: An investor who uses commonsense saving and investing methods in order to attain financial freedom.

asset: Anything that an individual or a corporation owns that has economic value to its owner.

asset class: A high-level classification of an investment. Examples of asset classes include stocks, bonds, cash, and real estate.

automatic deduction plan: Offered by brokers and mutual fund companies, whereby funds are transferred each month from a bank account and invested automatically.

back-end load: A commission or sales fee that is charged upon the redemption of mutual fund shares.

bond: A legal obligation of an issuing company or government to repay the principal of a loan to bond investors at a specified future date.

broker: An individual or firm that charges a fee or commission for executing buy and sell orders submitted by another individual or firm.

buy and hold: A long-term investing strategy in which an investor's stock portfolio is fully invested in the market all the time.

capital gain: An increase in the value of a capital asset such as common stock. If the asset is sold, the gain is a "realized" capital gain. A capital gain may be short term (one year or less) or long term (more than one year).

common stock: A class of stock in a company, normally with voting rights. Corporations may have several classes of common stock, as well as preferred stock, or they may have a single class of common stock. Common stock–holders are on the bottom of the ladder in a corporation's ownership structure, and have rights to a company's assets only after bond holders, preferred shareholders, and other debt holders have been satisfied.

compound interest: The way that fairly small amounts of money can grow substantially over time, as interest earns interest. Over time, the effect compounds to speed up the growth of your savings. The principle of "compound returns" refers to profits earned and reinvested in an investment portfolio.

contributions: Cash deposited into a retirement plan.

diversification: A risk management technique that mixes a wide variety of investments within a portfolio, thus minimizing the impact of any one security on overall portfolio performance.

dividend: A share of profits paid by a company to its investors. Not all companies pay dividends.

dollar cost averaging: The practice of steadily contributing a regular amount of money into an investment rather than one lump sum at once. Studies have shown that dollar cost averaging lowers risk and increases return over time.

equity: Another word for stock, or similar securities representing an ownership interest.

financial planner: An investment professional who helps individuals delineate financial plans with specific objectives and helps coordinate various financial concerns.

front-end load: A mutual fund commission or sales fee that is charged at the time shares are purchased. The load is added to the net asset value of the shares when calculating the public offering price.

index: A group of stocks that represents a market or a segment of a market. The Standard & Poor's 500 is the most well-known index, which measures the overall change in the value of the 500 stocks of the largest firms in the United States.

index fund: A mutual fund that only invests in the securities that make up a particular index.

investment: The process of buying property or securities with the intention that your holdings will increase in value.

IRA: Individual Retirement Account. A plan for retirement saving that allows assets to grow on a tax-deferred basis until the holder reaches retirement age.

Keogh plan: A qualified tax-deferred retirement plan for persons who are self-employed.

large-cap: Shorthand for "large capitalization," referring to very big publicly traded companies.

market capitalization: The total dollar value of all outstanding shares, calculated by multiplying the number of shares by the current market price.

mutual fund: An investment company that continuously offers new equity shares in an actively managed portfolio of securities. All shareholders participate in the gains or losses of the fund. Shares are issued and redeemed as per demand, and the fund's net asset value per share (NAV) is determined each day. The shares are redeemable on any business day at the net asset value. Each mutual fund's portfolio is invested to match the objective stated in the prospectus.

no-load fund: A mutual fund whose shares are sold without a commission or sales charge. The shares are distributed directly by the investment company.

portfolio: Any group of investments.

qualified distribution: A withdrawal from a retirement plan which is not subject to any penalties.

realized capital gain: A profit made on the sale of securities.

reinvestment: Using dividends, interest, and/or capital gains earned in an investment to purchase additional shares rather than receiving the distributions in cash.

return: The percentage of gain or loss for a security in a particular period, consisting of income plus capital gains relative to investment.

ROTH IRA: A type of Individual Retirement Account that doesn't offer a tax deduction on contributions, but allows the withdrawal of funds on a tax-free basis upon reaching retirement age.

routing number: Used by banks to identify where checks should be sent for processing and clearing.

SEP IRA: Simplified Employee Pension (SEP) IRA. A retirement plan for self-employed individuals and small companies.

small-cap: Shorthand for "small capitalization," referring to small publicly traded companies.

take-home pay: The amount of your paycheck after taxes and other withholdings.

unrealized capital gain: An increase in the value of securities that you currently own and have not sold.

INDEX

Page numbers in *italics* indicate charts.